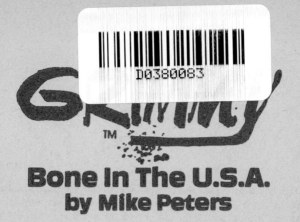

GRIMMY ™

Bone In The U.S.A.
by Mike Peters

TOR ®

A TOM DOHERTY ASSOCIATES BOOK
NEW YORK

MOTHER GOOSE AND GRIMM: BONE IN THE USA

TM and Copyright © 1992 Grimmy, Inc. Licensed by MGM/UA.

A Tor Book
Published by Tom Doherty Associates, Inc.
49 West 24th Street
New York, N.Y. 10010

ISBN: 0-812-51526-9

First Tor edition: January 1992

Printed in the United States of America

0 9 8 7 6 5 4

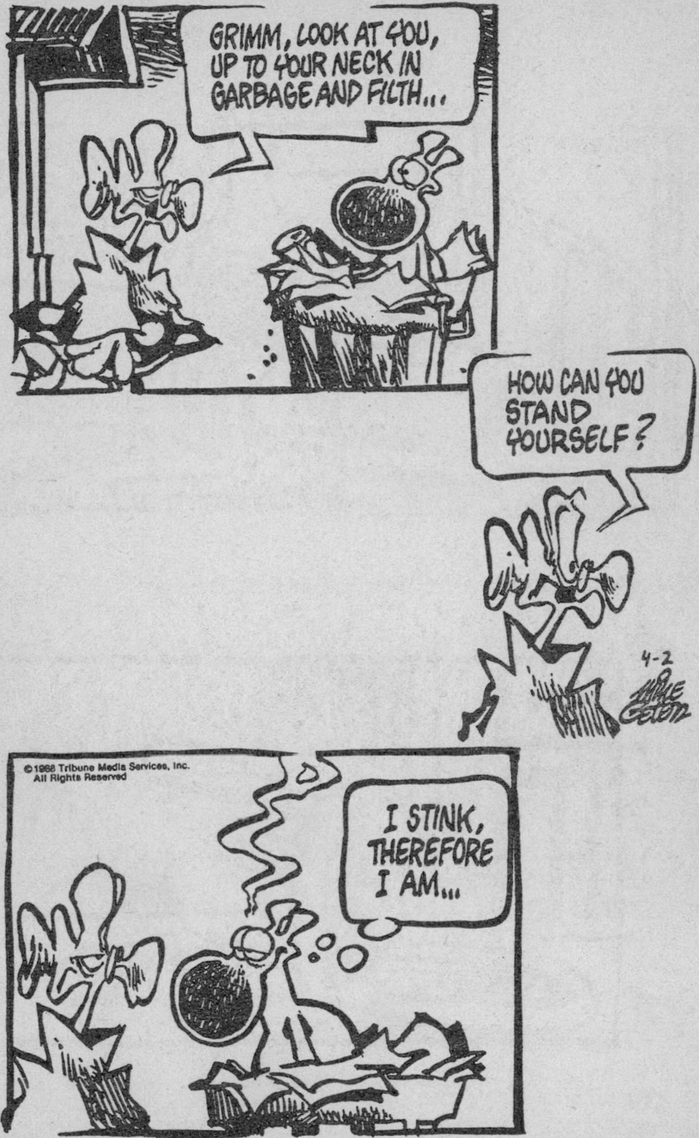
GRIMM, LOOK AT YOU, UP TO YOUR NECK IN GARBAGE AND FILTH...
HOW CAN YOU STAND YOURSELF?
4-2
MIKE PETERS
I STINK, THEREFORE I AM...

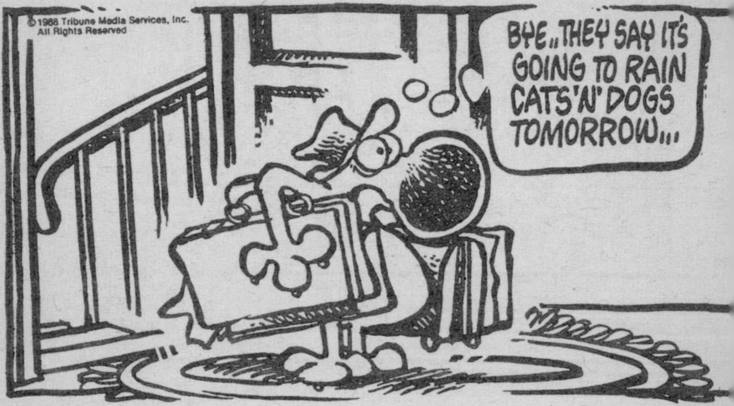
© 1988 Tribune Media Services, Inc.
All Rights Reserved
BYE.. THEY SAY IT'S GOING TO RAIN CATS 'N' DOGS TOMORROW...

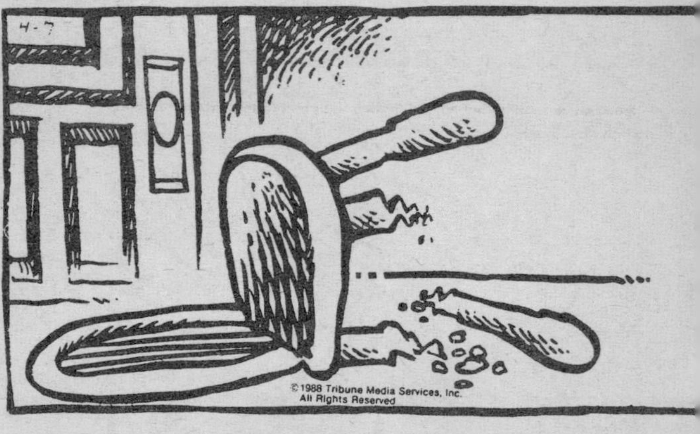
4-7
© 1988 Tribune Media Services, Inc.
All Rights Reserved

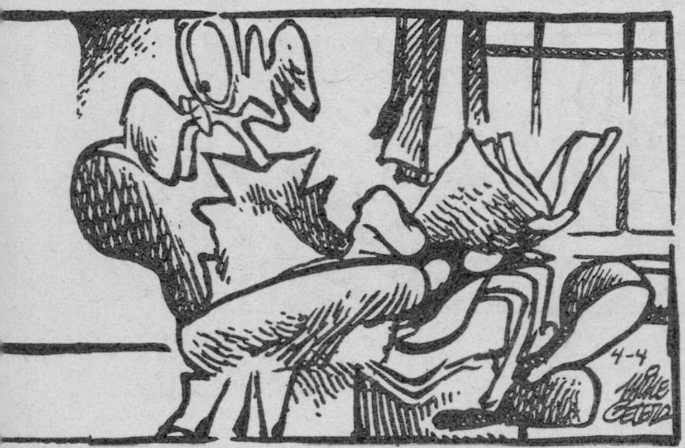
4-4
MIKE PETERS

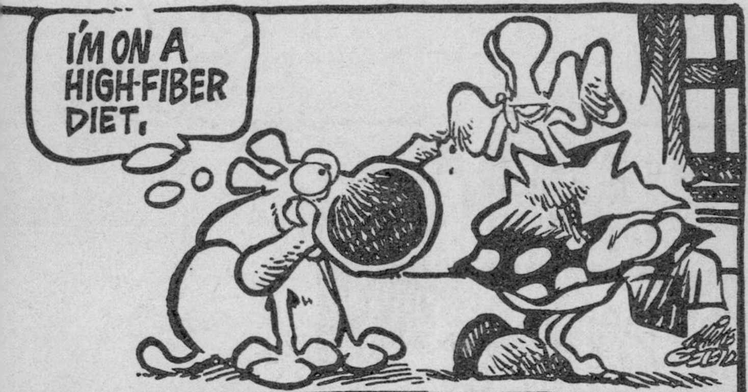
I'M ON A HIGH-FIBER DIET.
MIKE PETERS

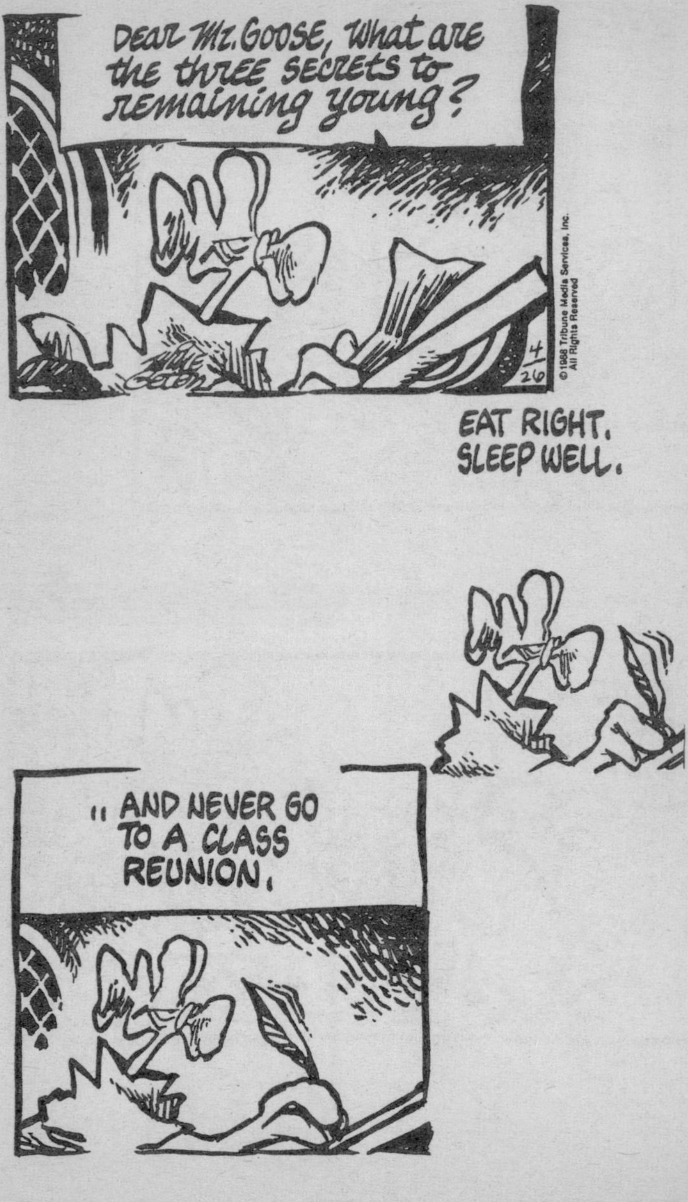
DEAR MR. GOOSE, What are the three SECRETS to remaining young?
© 1988 Tribune Media Services, Inc. All Rights Reserved
4/26
EAT RIGHT. SLEEP WELL.
.. AND NEVER GO TO A CLASS REUNION.

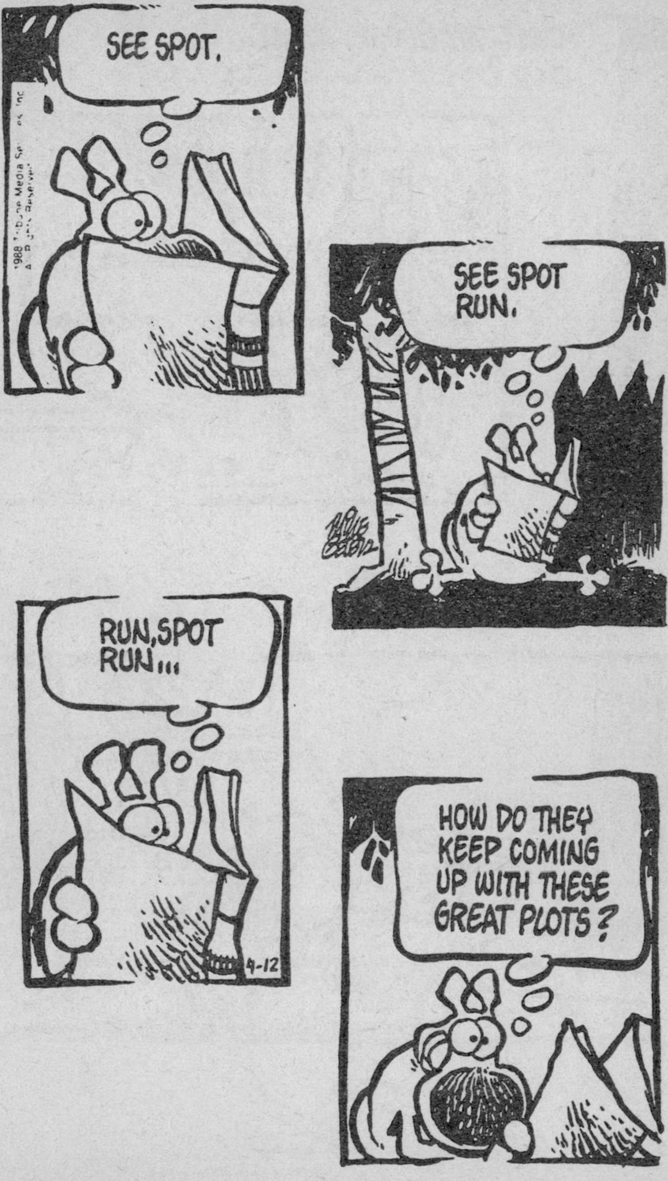
SEE SPOT.
SEE SPOT RUN.
RUN, SPOT RUN...
4-12
HOW DO THEY KEEP COMING UP WITH THESE GREAT PLOTS?

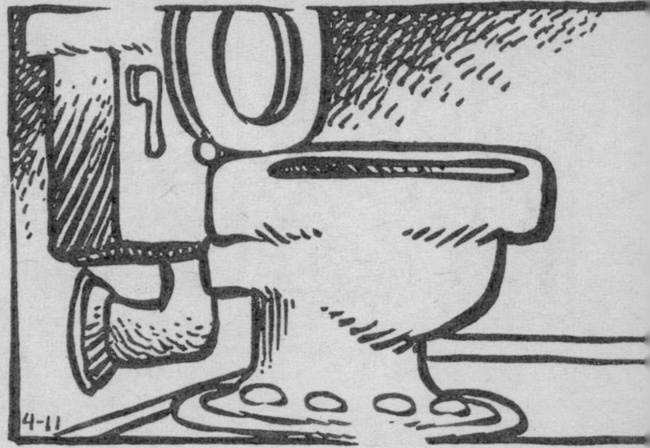
4-11

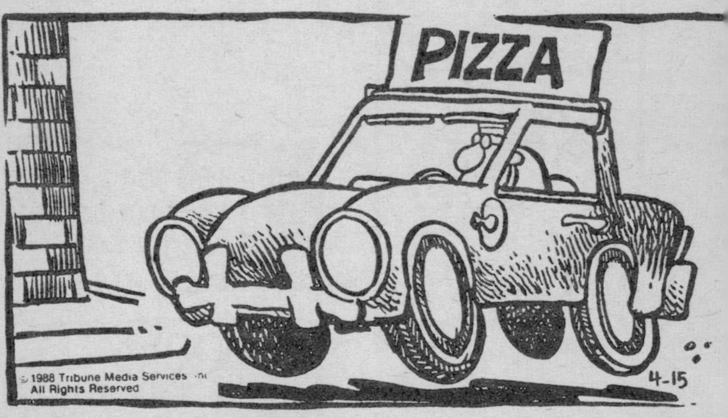
PIZZA
4-15

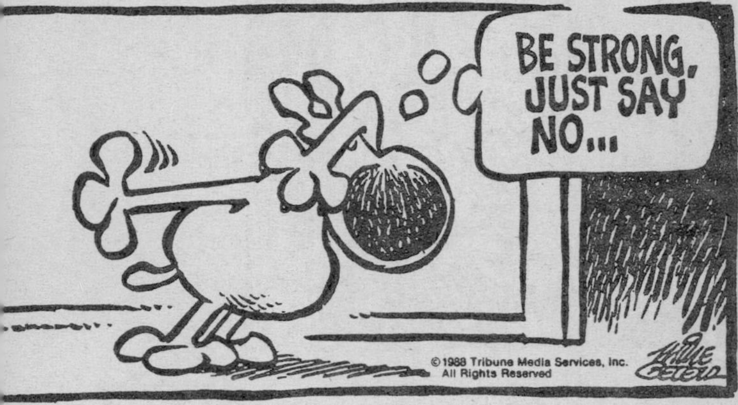
BE STRONG, JUST SAY NO...
©1988 Tribune Media Services, Inc.
All Rights Reserved

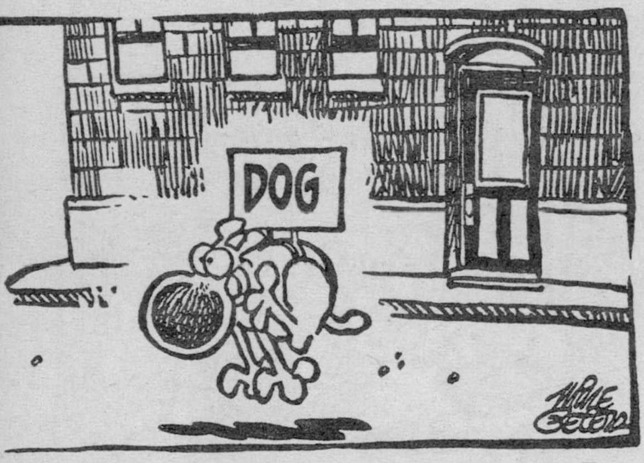
DOG

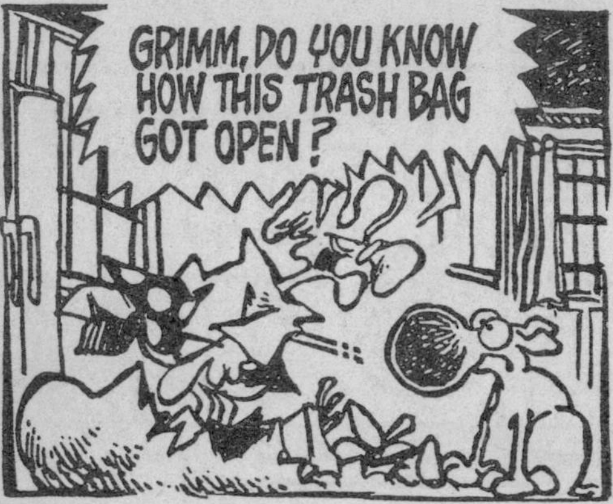
GRIMM, DO YOU KNOW HOW THIS TRASH BAG GOT OPEN ?

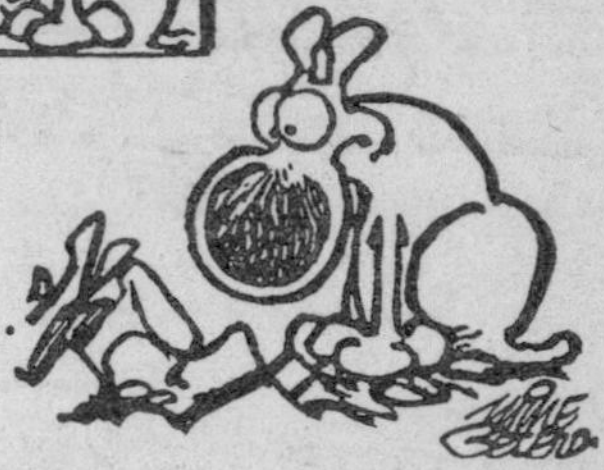

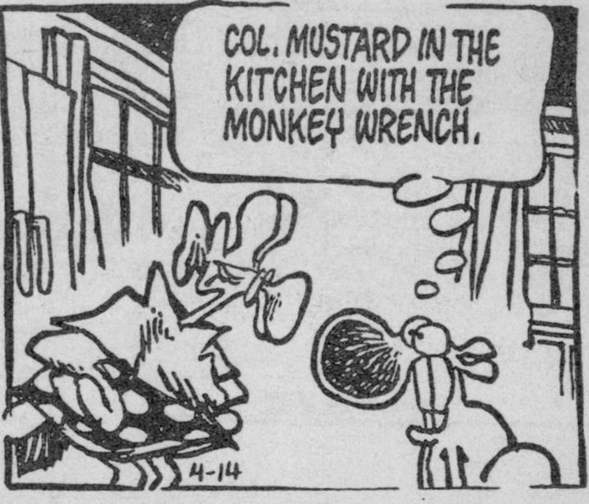
COL. MUSTARD IN THE KITCHEN WITH THE MONKEY WRENCH.
4-14

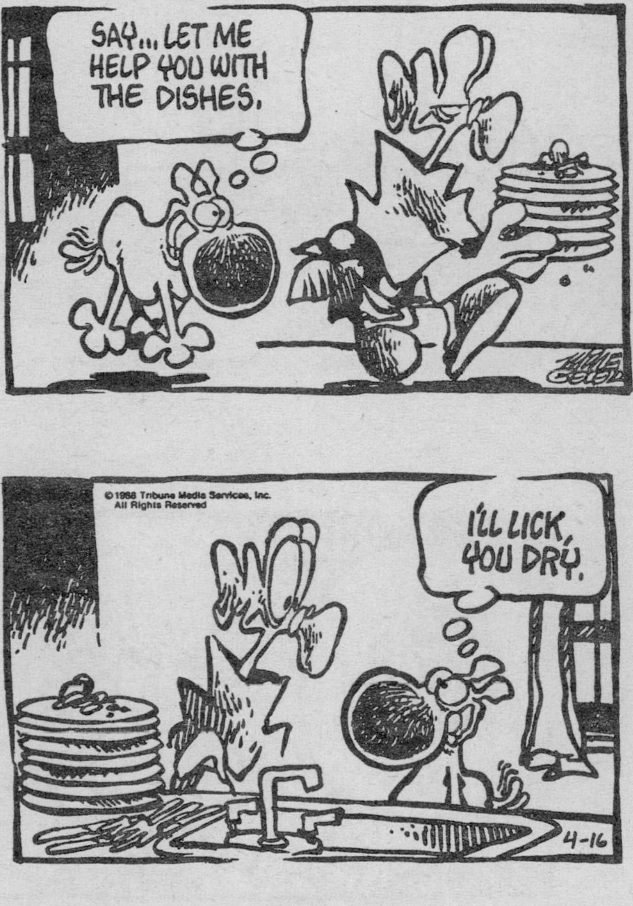
SAY... LET ME HELP YOU WITH THE DISHES.
© 1986 Tribune Media Services, Inc. All Rights Reserved
I'LL LICK, YOU DRY.
4-16

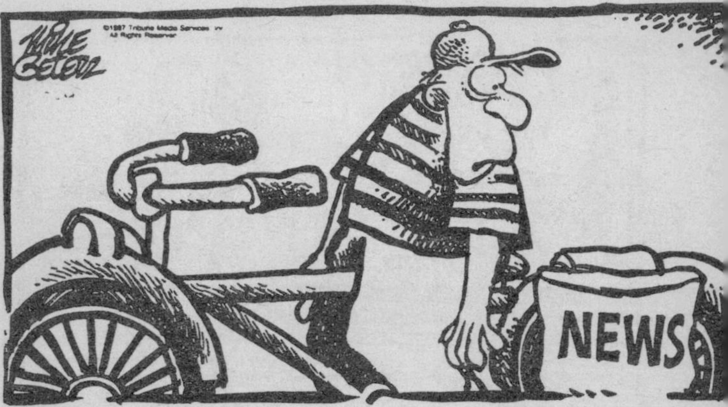
©1987 Tribune Media Services
All Rights Reserved
NEWS

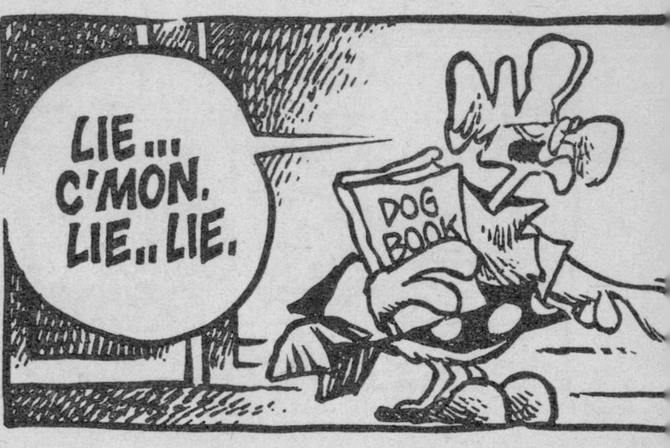
LIE... C'MON. LIE.. LIE.
DOG BOOK

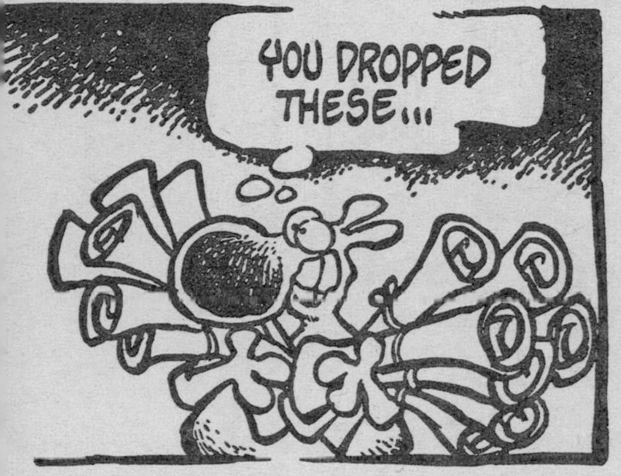
YOU DROPPED THESE...

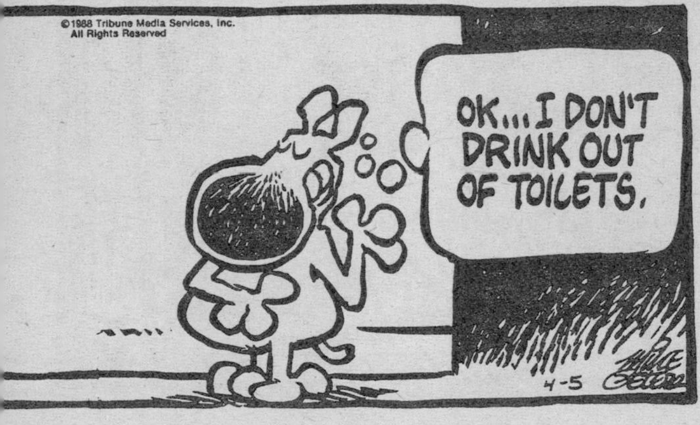
©1988 Tribune Media Services, Inc.
All Rights Reserved
OK...I DON'T DRINK OUT OF TOILETS.
4-5

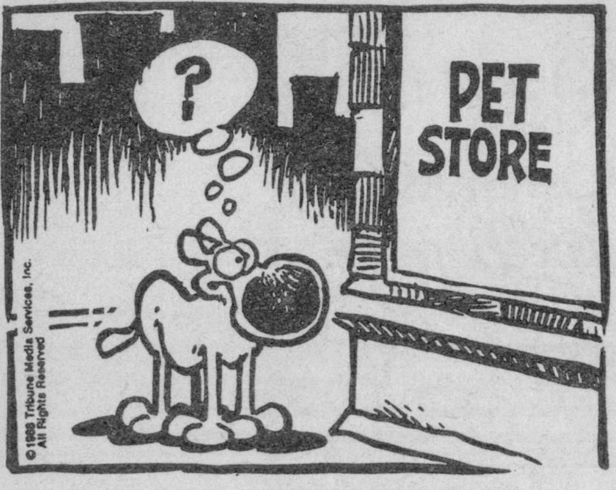
?
PET
STORE
© 1988 Tribune Media Services, Inc.
All Rights Reserved

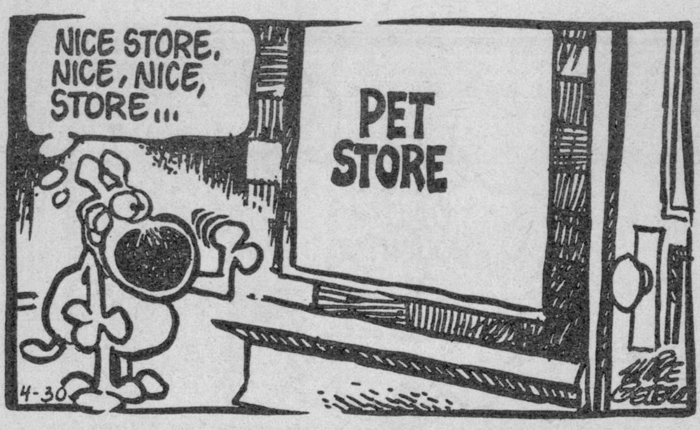
NICE STORE,
NICE, NICE,
STORE...
PET
STORE
4-30

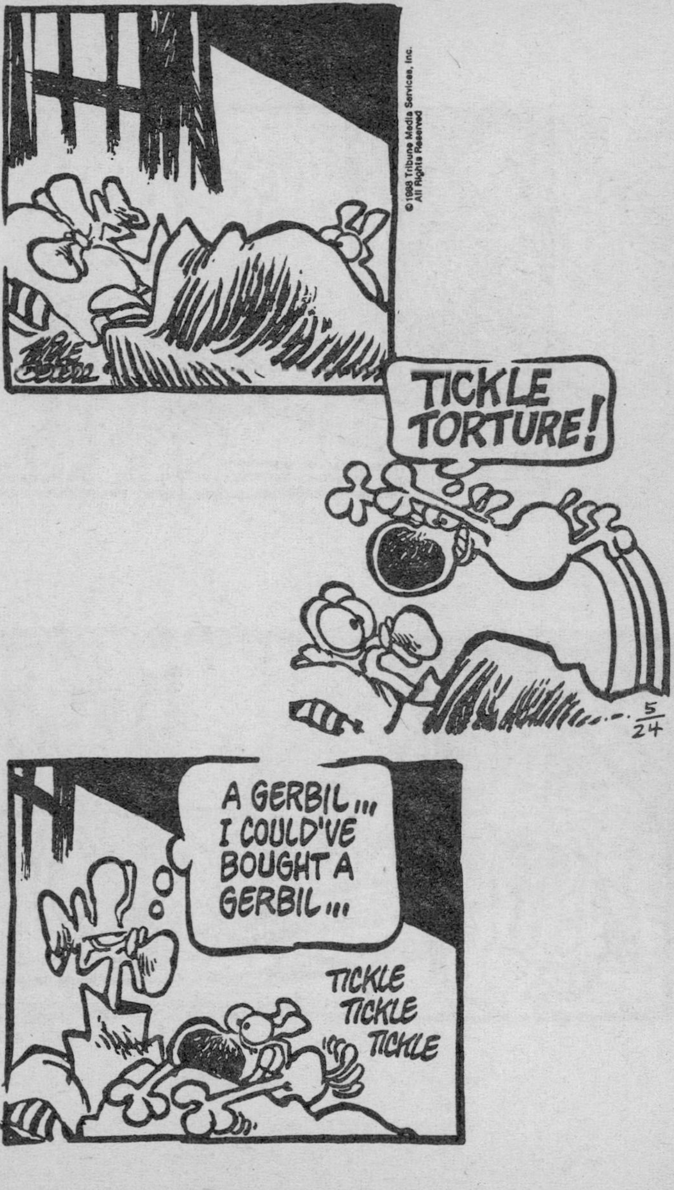
© 1988 Tribune Media Services, Inc.
All Rights Reserved
TICKLE TORTURE!
5/24
A GERBIL... I COULD'VE BOUGHT A GERBIL...
TICKLE
TICKLE
TICKLE

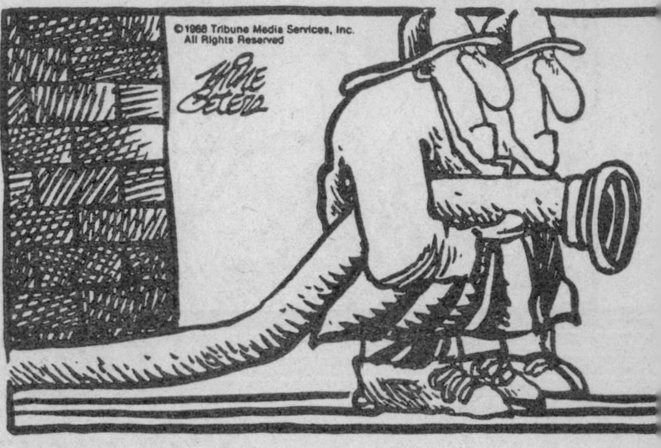
©1988 Tribune Media Services, Inc.
All Rights Reserved

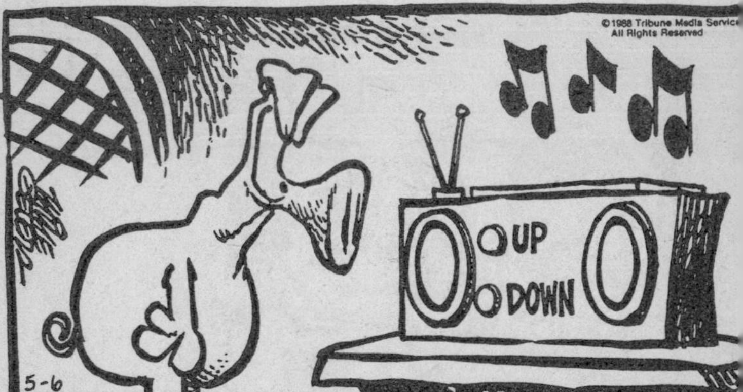
©1988 Tribune Media Servic
All Rights Reserved
UP
DOWN
5-6

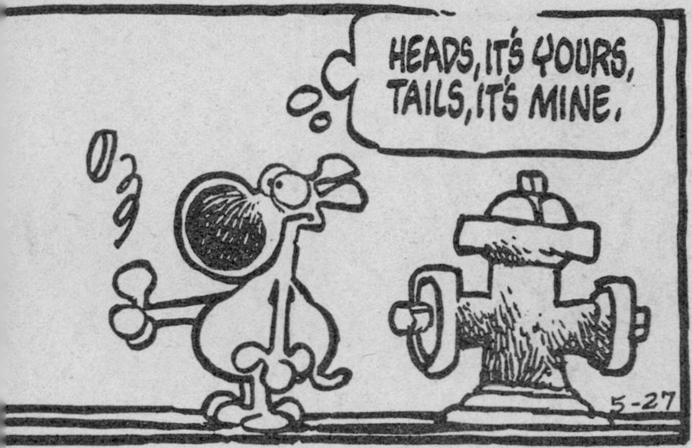
HEADS, IT'S YOURS, TAILS, IT'S MINE.
5-27

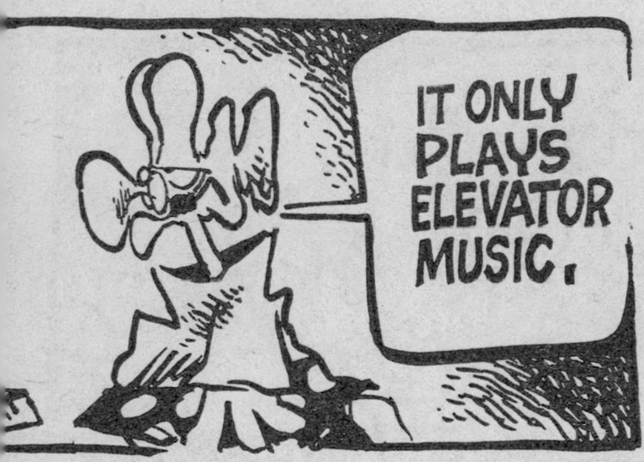
IT ONLY PLAYS ELEVATOR MUSIC.

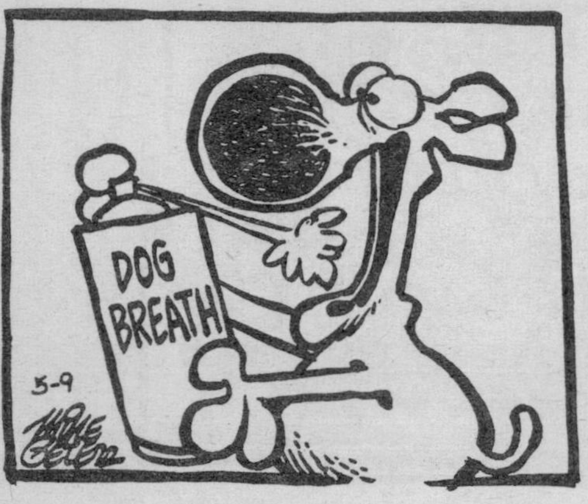
DOG BREATH
5-9

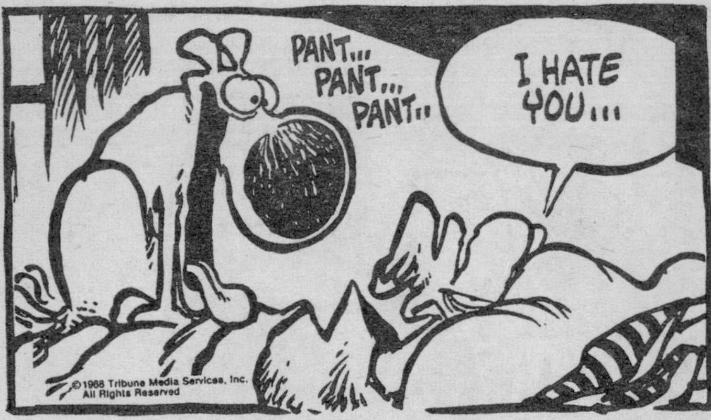
PANT... PANT... PANT..
I HATE YOU...
©1988 Tribune Media Services, Inc.
All Rights Reserved

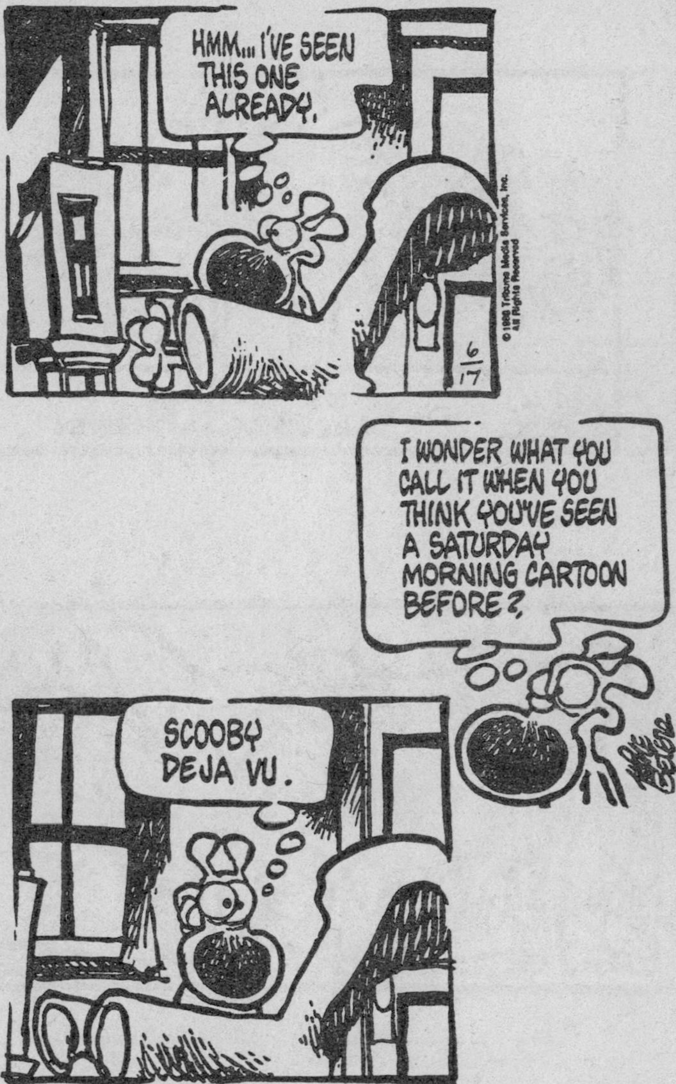

HMM... I'VE SEEN THIS ONE ALREADY.
6/17
I WONDER WHAT YOU CALL IT WHEN YOU THINK YOU'VE SEEN A SATURDAY MORNING CARTOON BEFORE?
SCOOBY DEJA VU.

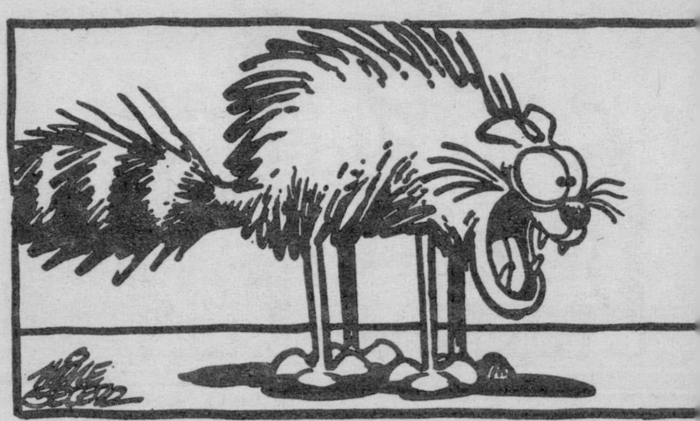

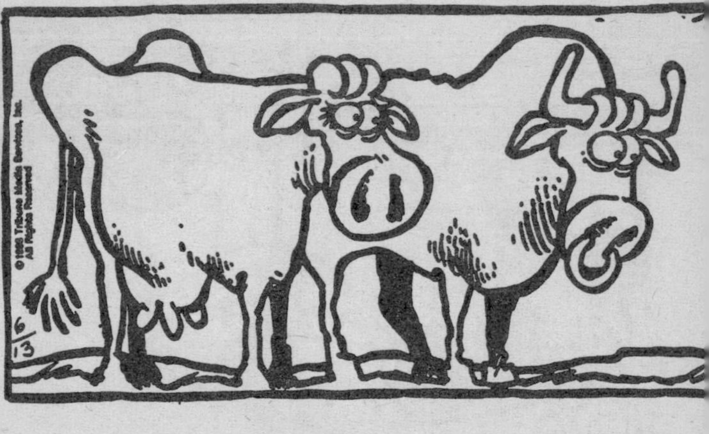
Tribune Media Services, Inc.
All Rights Reserved
6/13

WHOA,,, LIKE I FEEL AN AURA OF INTENSE HOSTILITY HERE.

© 1998 Tribune Media Services, Inc.
All Rights Reserved

6-15

SO...THIS IS YOUR SIGNIFICANT UDDER.

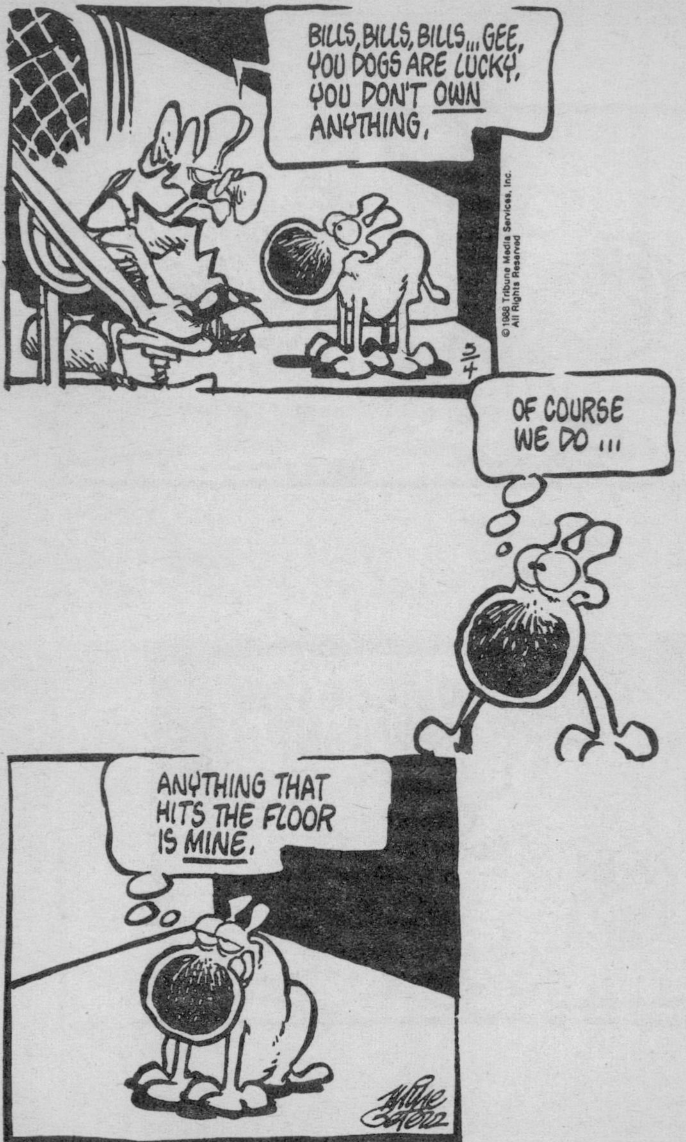
BILLS, BILLS, BILLS... GEE, YOU DOGS ARE LUCKY, YOU DON'T OWN ANYTHING.
© 1988 Tribune Media Services, Inc. All Rights Reserved
5/4
OF COURSE WE DO ...
ANYTHING THAT HITS THE FLOOR IS MINE.

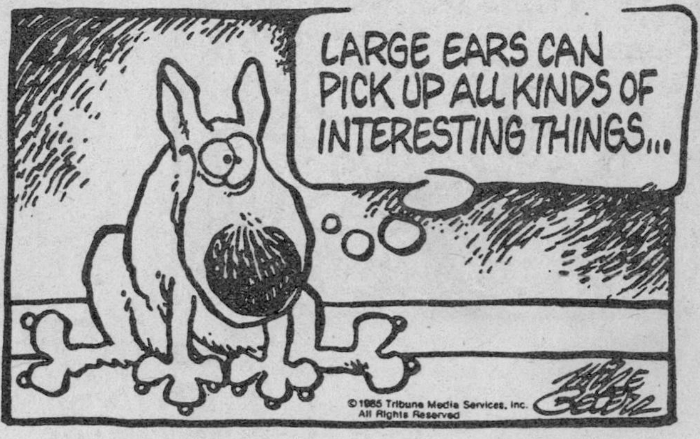
LARGE EARS CAN PICK UP ALL KINDS OF INTERESTING THINGS...
©1985 Tribune Media Services, Inc.
All Rights Reserved

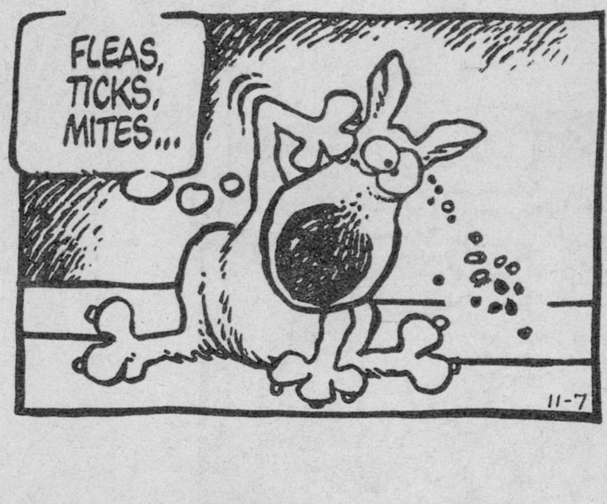
FLEAS, TICKS, MITES...
11-7

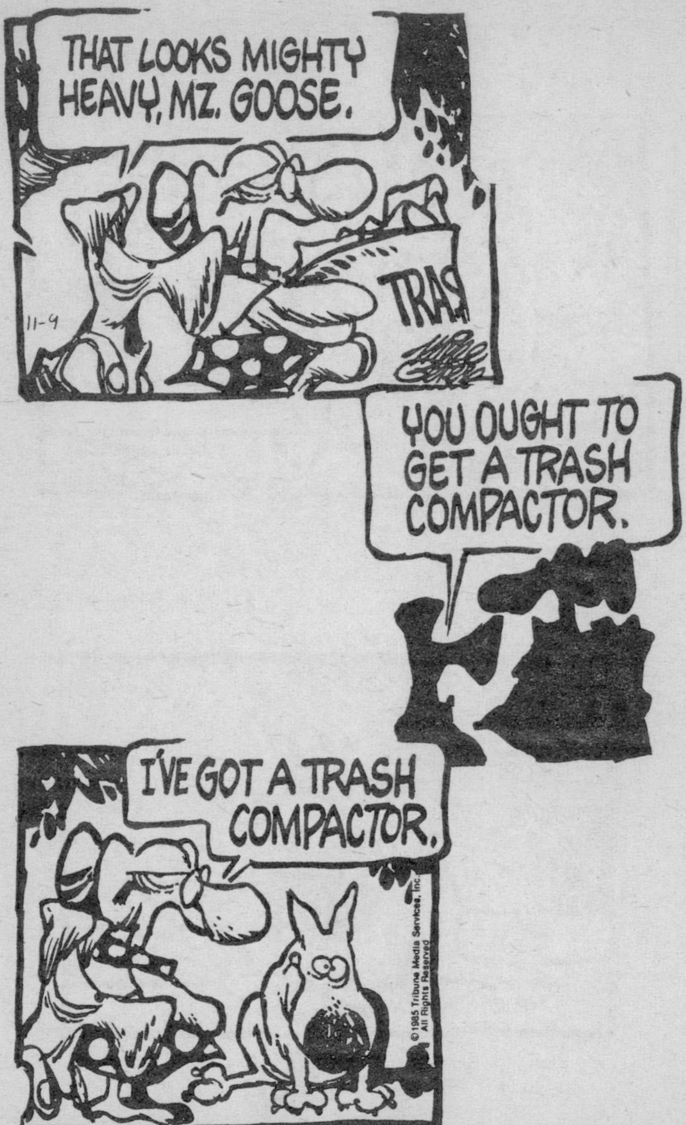
THAT LOOKS MIGHTY HEAVY, MZ. GOOSE.
TRAS
11-9
YOU OUGHT TO GET A TRASH COMPACTOR.
I'VE GOT A TRASH COMPACTOR.
© 1985 Tribune Media Services, Inc. All Rights Reserved

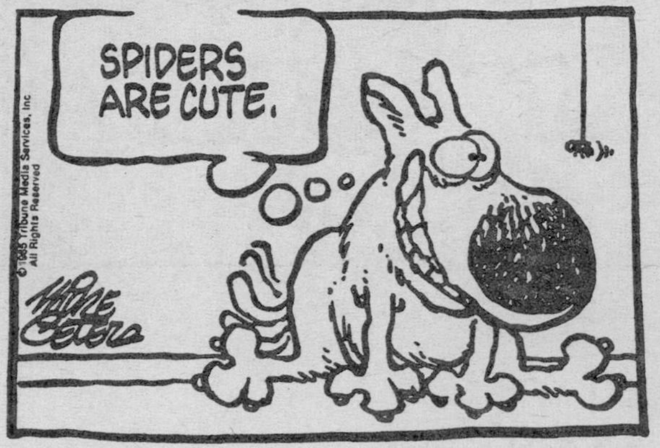
SPIDERS ARE CUTE.
©1985 Tribune Media Services, Inc
All Rights Reserved

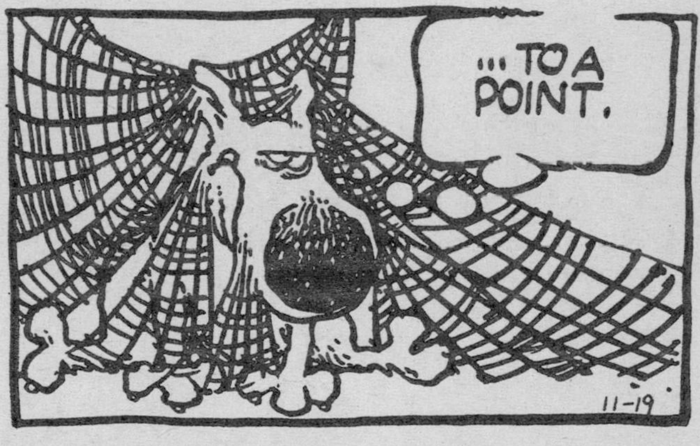
...TO A POINT.
11-19

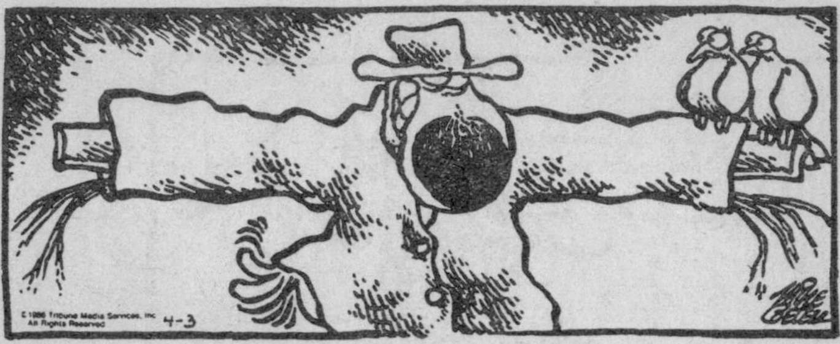
© 1986 Tribune Media Services, Inc
All Rights Reserved
4-3

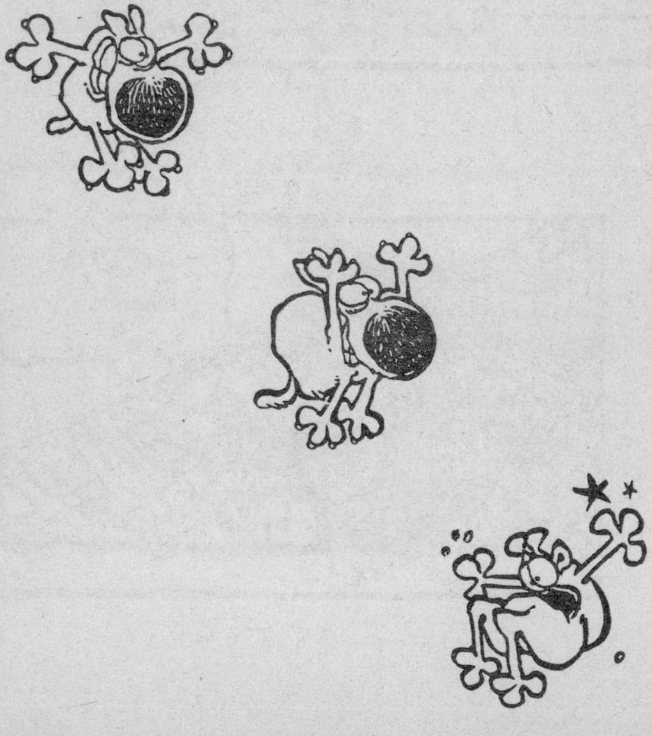

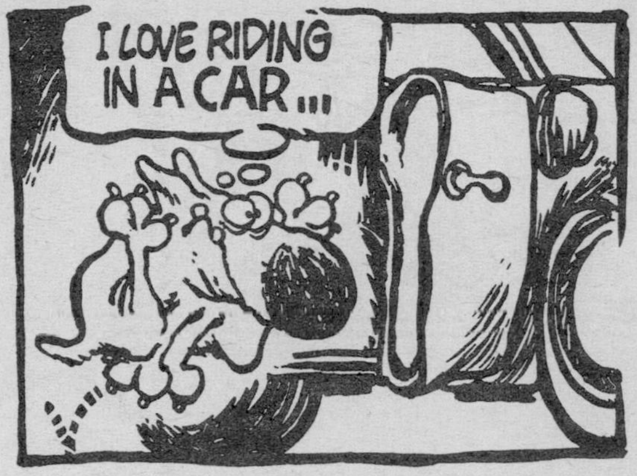
I LOVE RIDING IN A CAR...

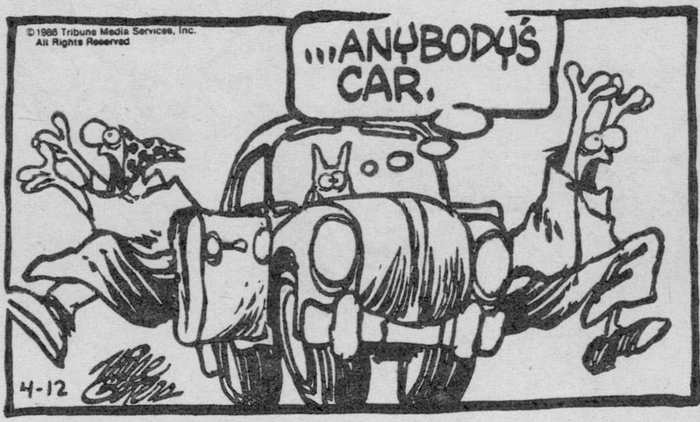
© 1988 Tribune Media Services, Inc.
All Rights Reserved
...ANYBODY'S CAR.
4-12

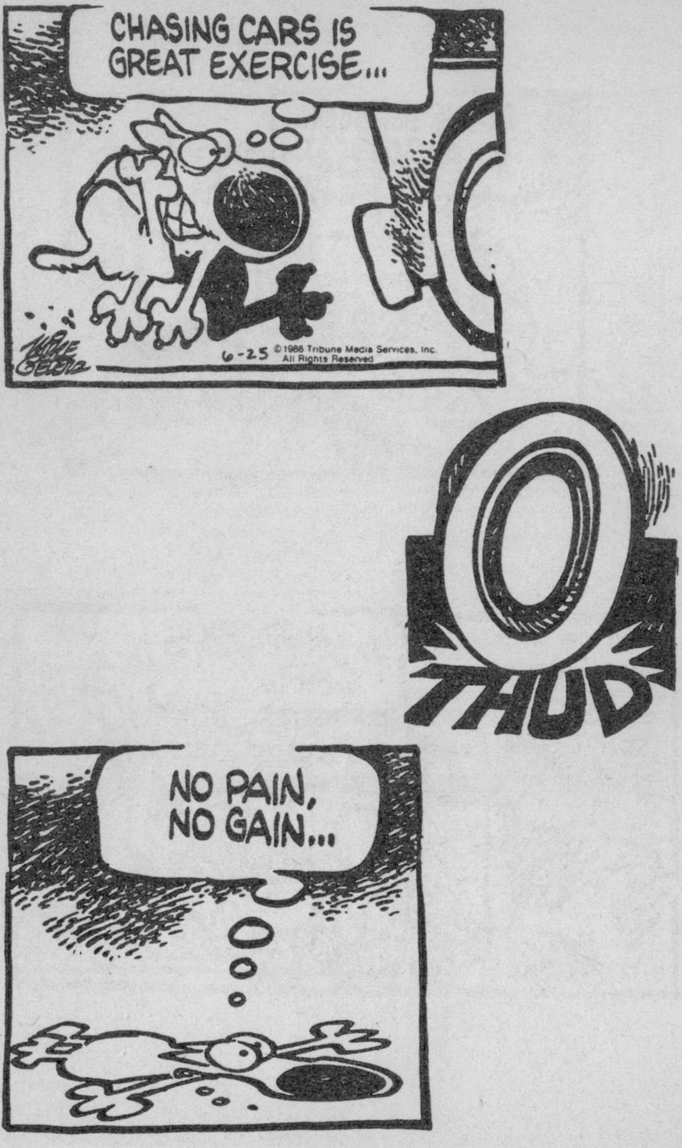
CHASING CARS IS GREAT EXERCISE...
6-25
© 1986 Tribune Media Services, Inc. All Rights Reserved
THUD
NO PAIN, NO GAIN...

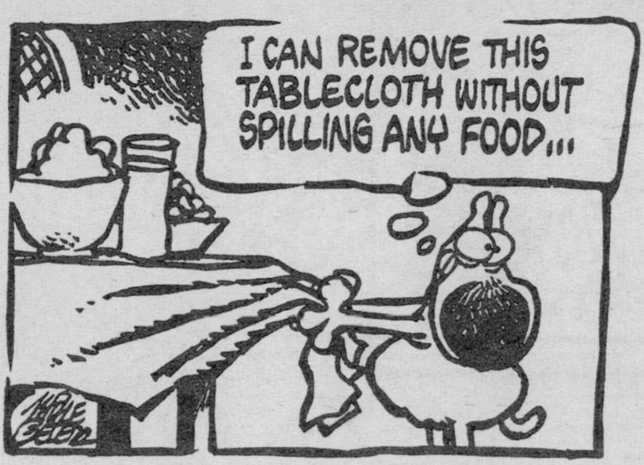
I CAN REMOVE THIS TABLECLOTH WITHOUT SPILLING ANY FOOD...

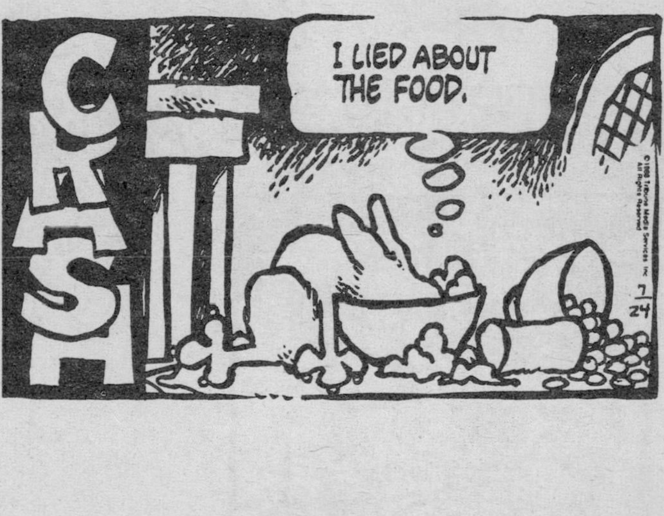
CRASH
I LIED ABOUT THE FOOD.
© 1988 Tribune Media Services, Inc. All Rights Reserved
7/24

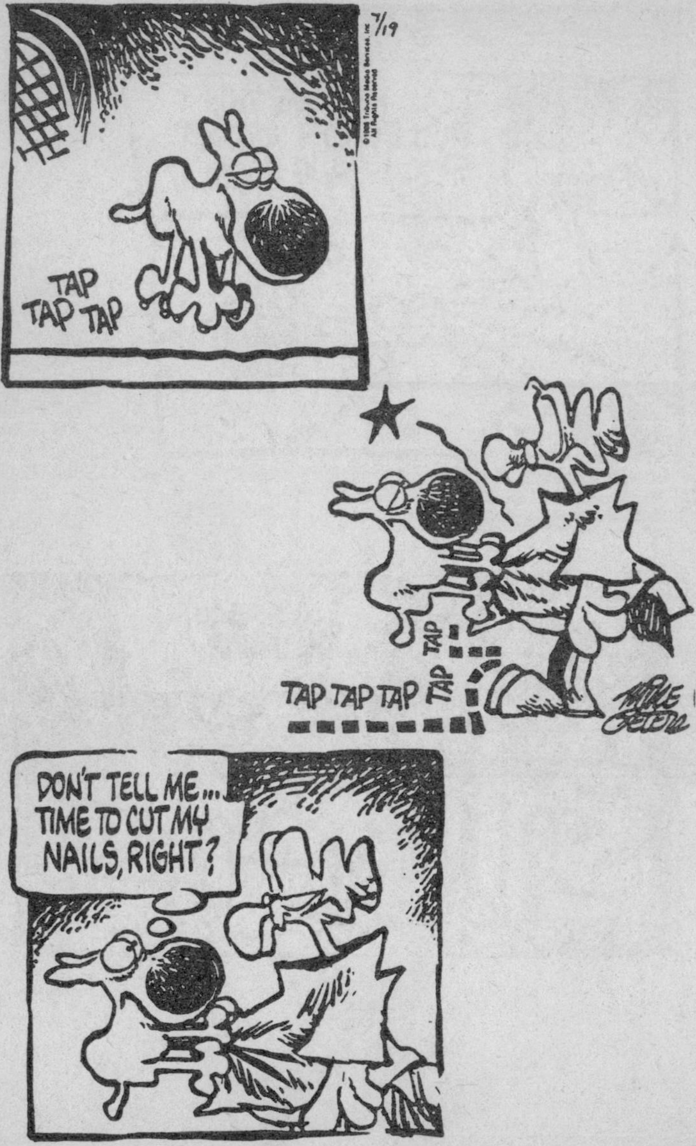
TAP
TAP TAP
7/19
TAP TAP TAP TAP TAP
DON'T TELL ME... TIME TO CUT MY NAILS, RIGHT?

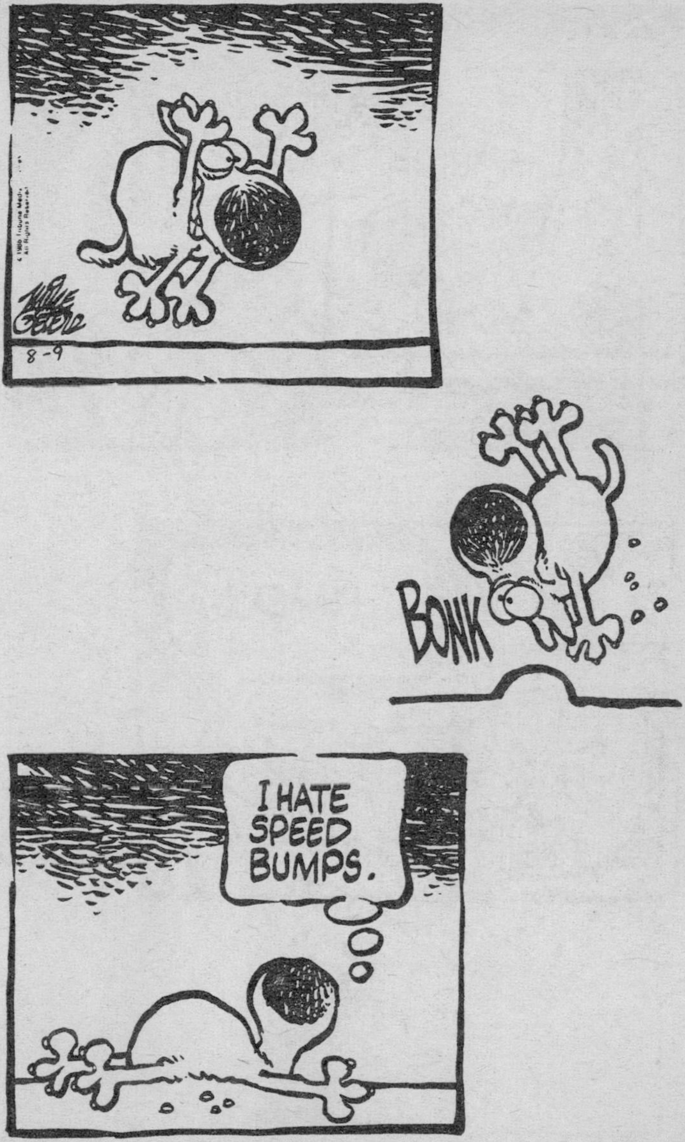
8-9
BONK
I HATE SPEED BUMPS.

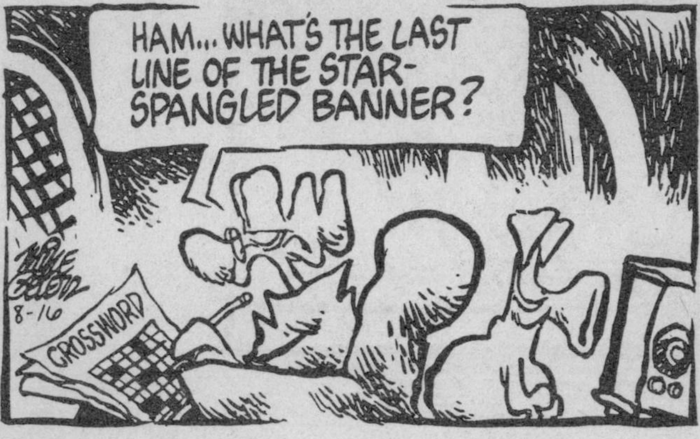
HAM... WHAT'S THE LAST LINE OF THE STAR-SPANGLED BANNER?
8-16
CROSSWORD

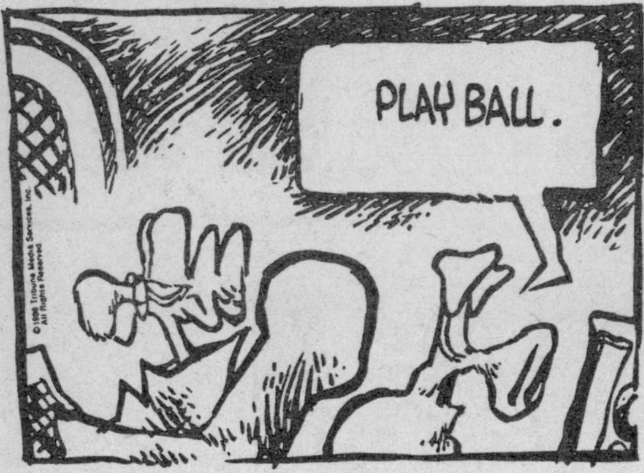
PLAY BALL.
©1988 Tribune Media Services, Inc.
All Rights Reserved

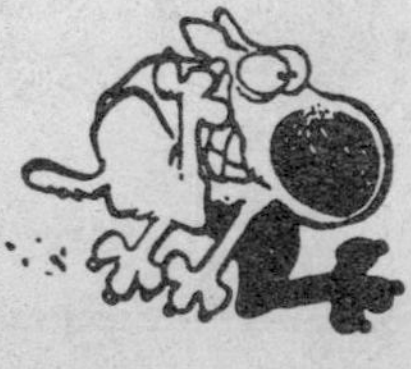

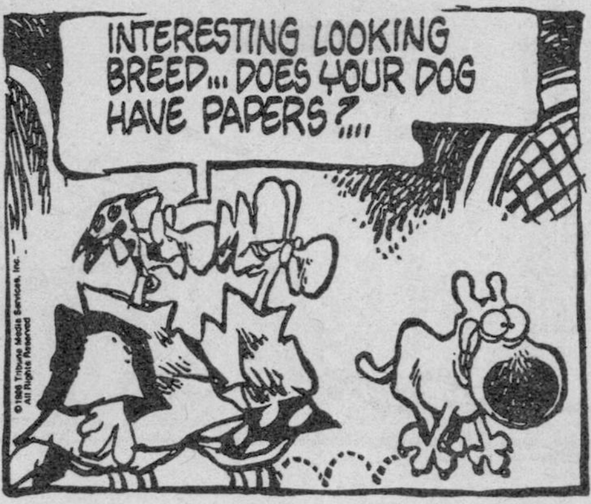
INTERESTING LOOKING BREED... DOES YOUR DOG HAVE PAPERS?....
©1988 Tribune Media Services, Inc. All Rights Reserved

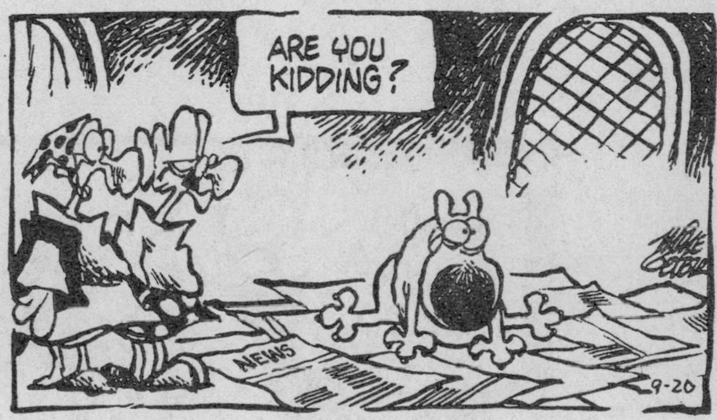
ARE YOU KIDDING?
NEWS
9-20

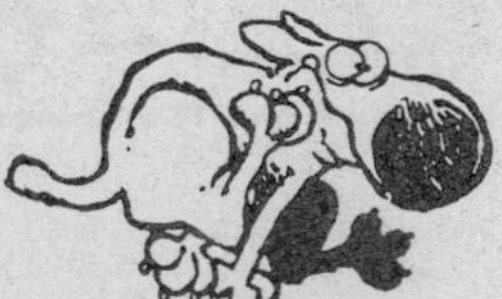

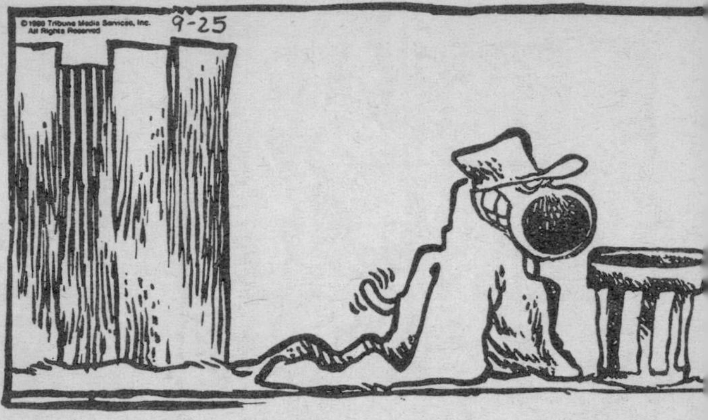
©1988 Tribune Media Services, Inc.
All Rights Reserved
9-25

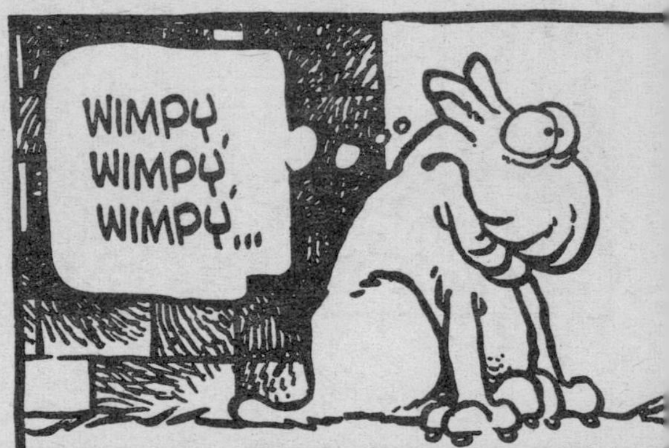
WIMPY, WIMPY, WIMPY...

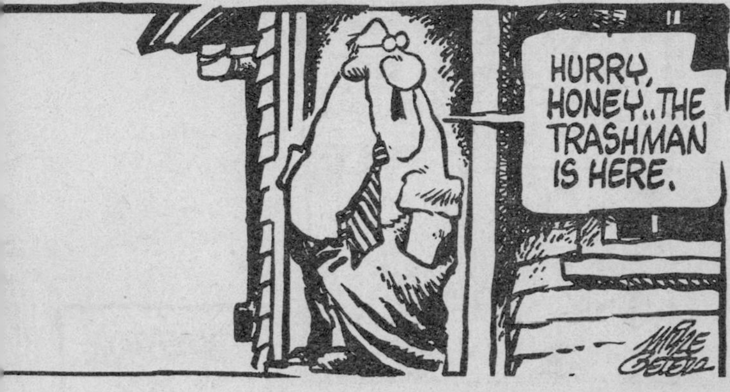
HURRY, HONEY.. THE TRASHMAN IS HERE.

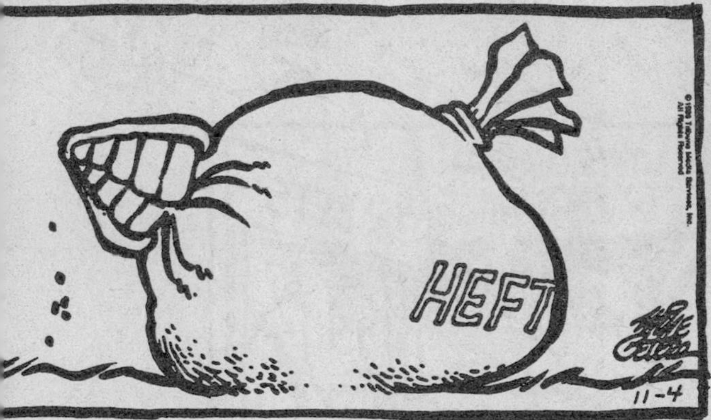
HEFT
11-4

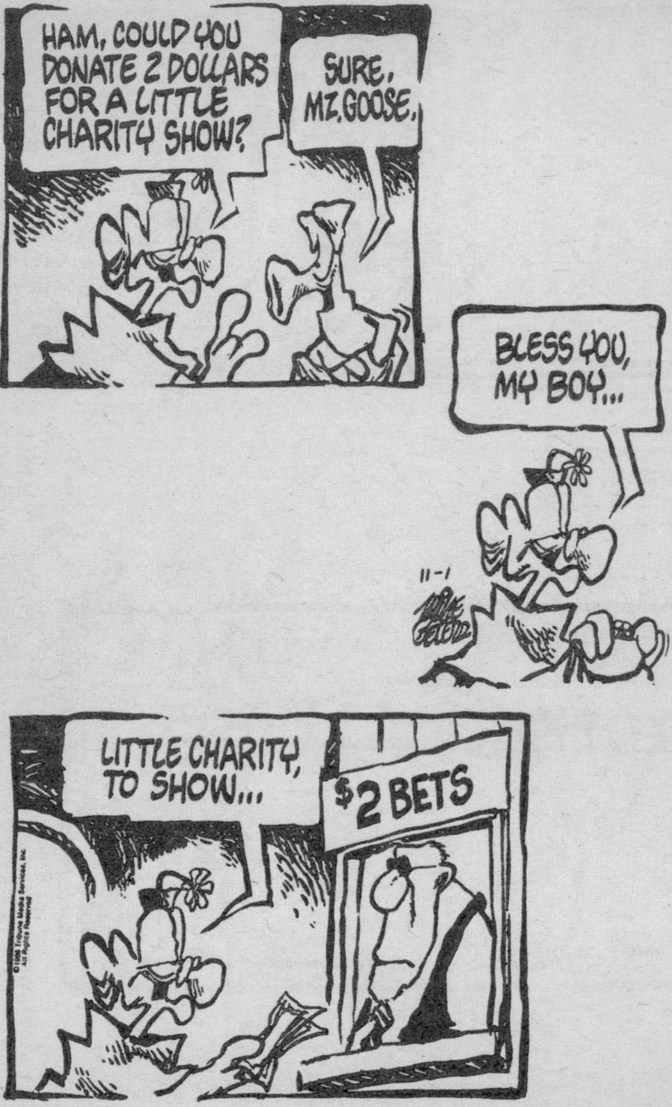
HAM, COULD YOU DONATE 2 DOLLARS FOR A LITTLE CHARITY SHOW?
SURE, MZ. GOOSE.
BLESS YOU, MY BOY...
LITTLE CHARITY, TO SHOW...
$2 BETS

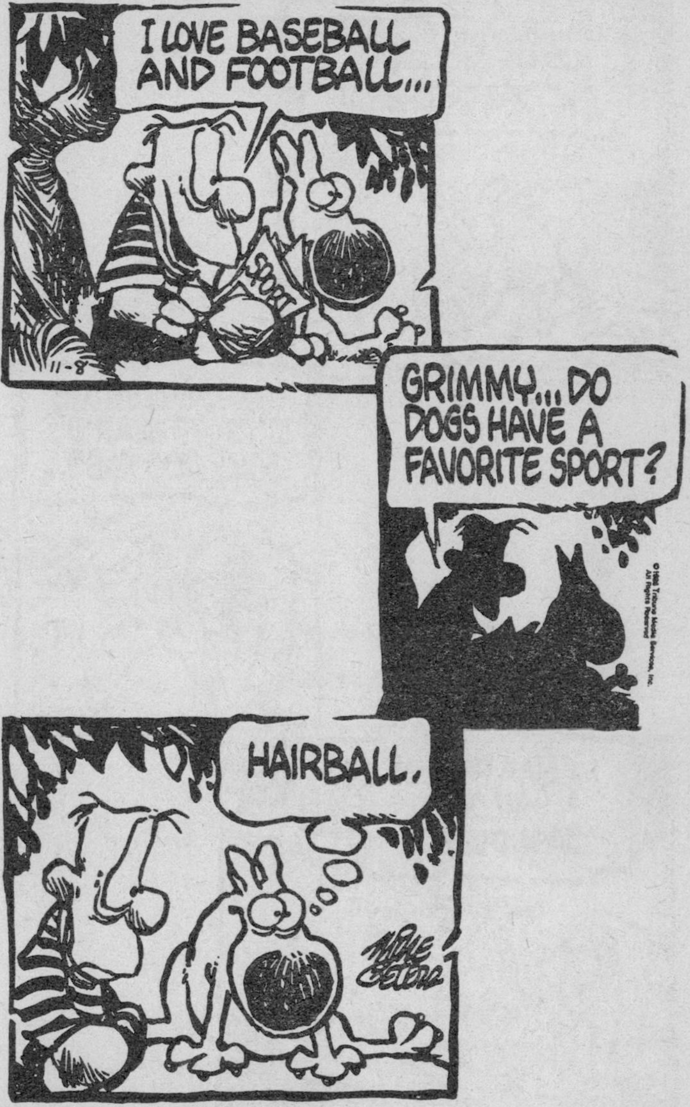
I LOVE BASEBALL AND FOOTBALL...
SPORT
11-8
GRIMMY... DO DOGS HAVE A FAVORITE SPORT?
Tribune Media Services, Inc.
All Rights Reserved
HAIRBALL.
MIKE PETERS

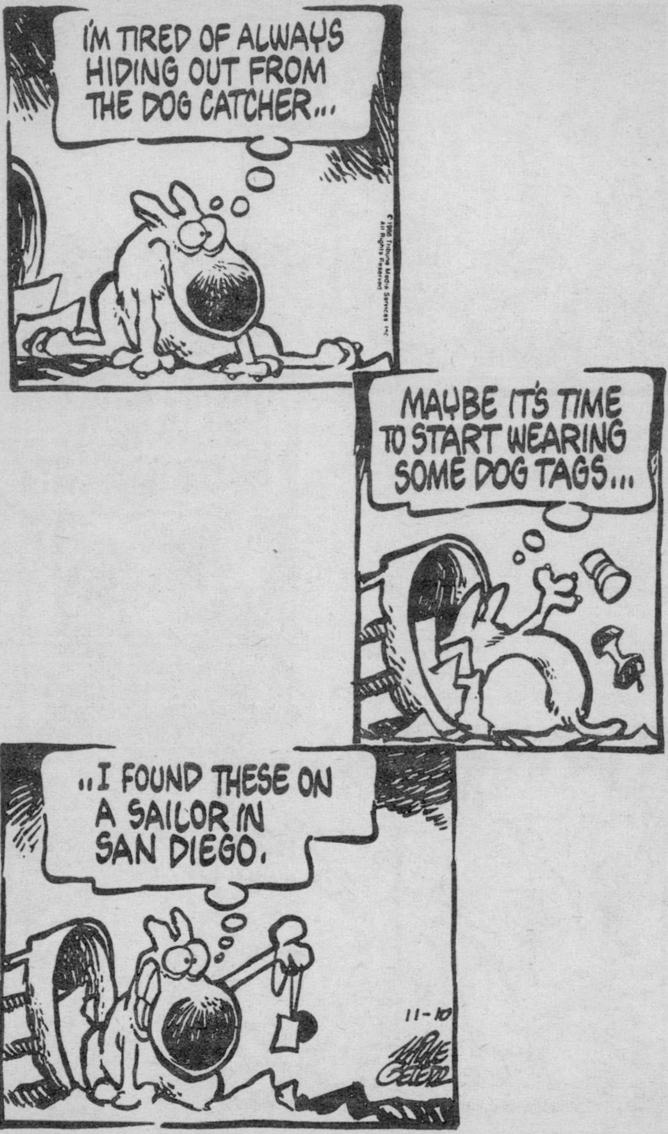

I'M TIRED OF ALWAYS HIDING OUT FROM THE DOG CATCHER...
MAYBE IT'S TIME TO START WEARING SOME DOG TAGS...
..I FOUND THESE ON A SAILOR IN SAN DIEGO.
11-10

CHOW DOWN!
GRIM
GULP
GRIM
TOO TIGHT... MY... COLLAR... TOO TIGHT...

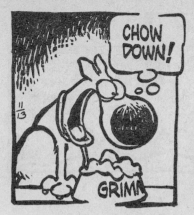

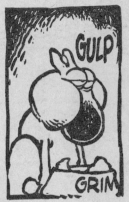

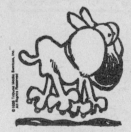

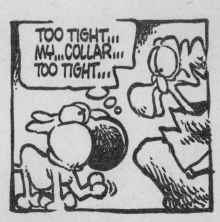

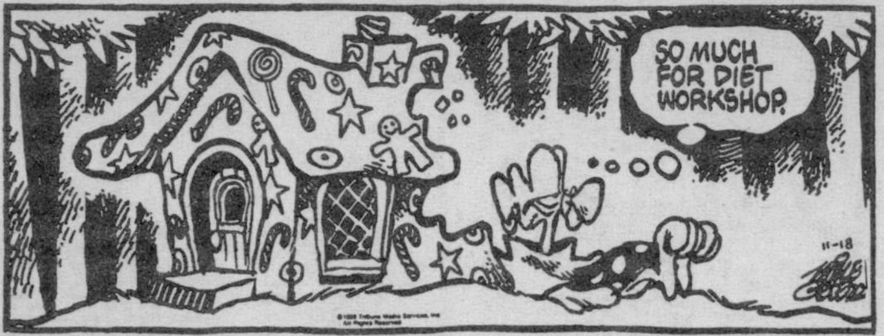
SO MUCH FOR DIET WORKSHOP.
11-18

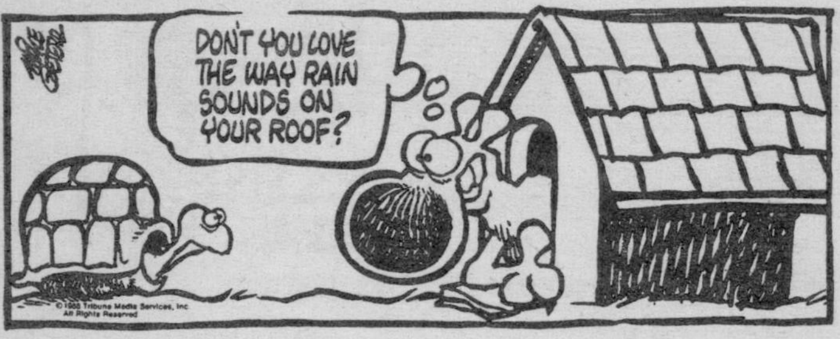
DON'T YOU LOVE THE WAY RAIN SOUNDS ON YOUR ROOF?
© 1988 Tribune Media Services, Inc. All Rights Reserved

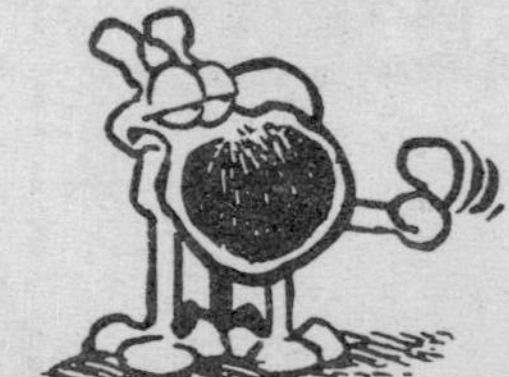

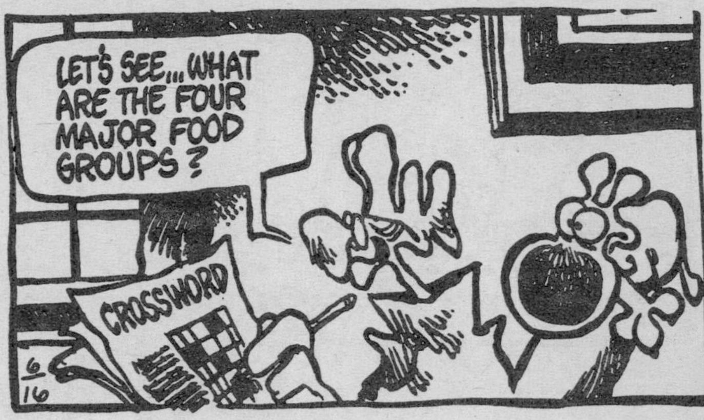
LET'S SEE... WHAT ARE THE FOUR MAJOR FOOD GROUPS ?
CROSSWORD
6/16

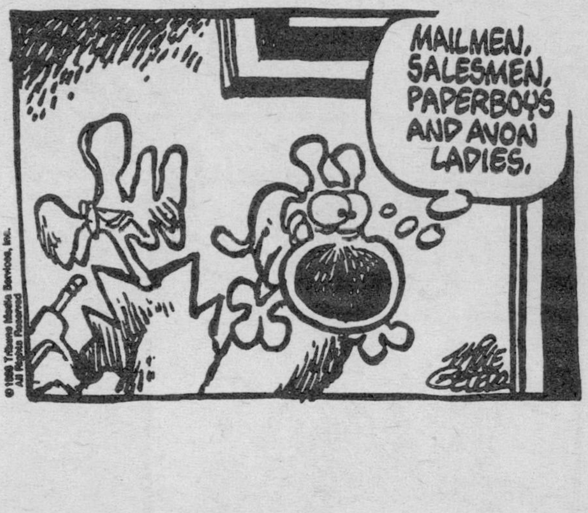
MAILMEN, SALESMEN, PAPERBOYS AND AVON LADIES.

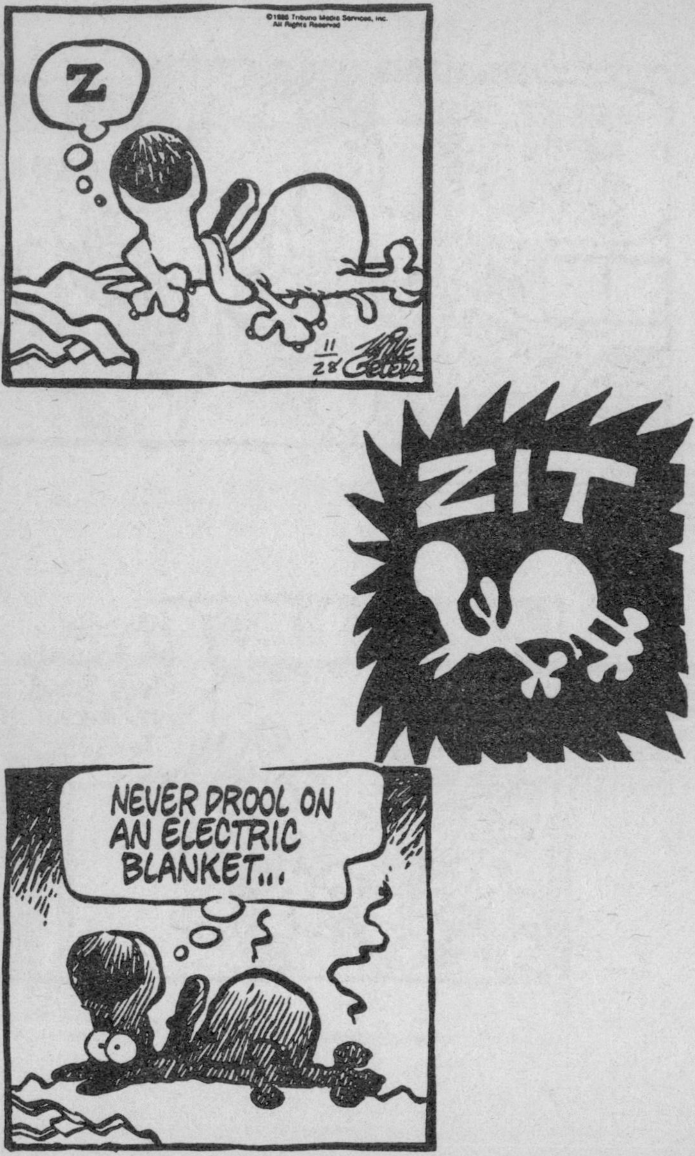
Z
ZIT
NEVER DROOL ON AN ELECTRIC BLANKET...

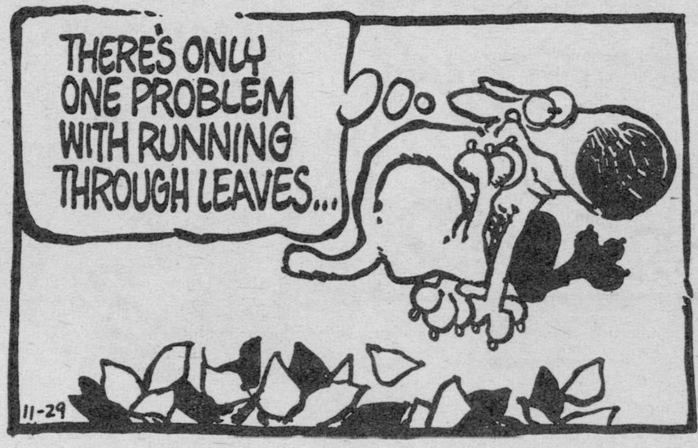
THERE'S ONLY ONE PROBLEM WITH RUNNING THROUGH LEAVES...
11-29

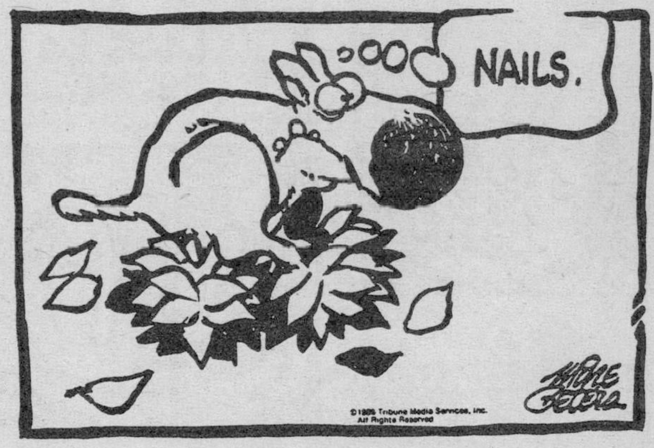
NAILS.
Tribune Media Services, Inc.
All Rights Reserved

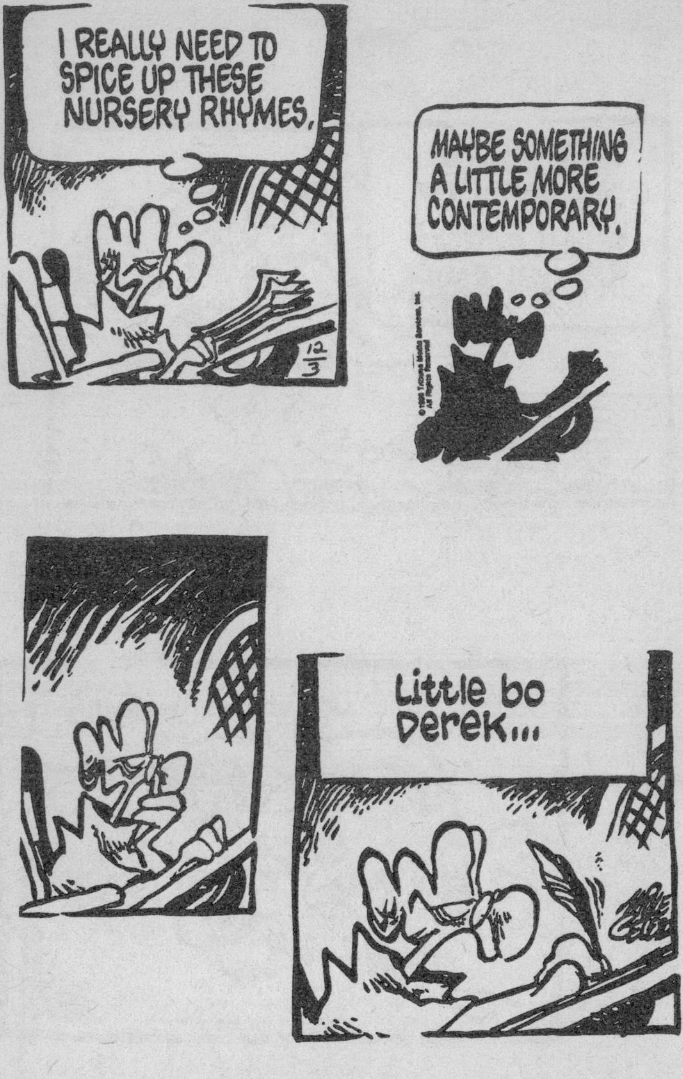
I REALLY NEED TO SPICE UP THESE NURSERY RHYMES.
12/3
MAYBE SOMETHING A LITTLE MORE CONTEMPORARY.
Little bo Derek...

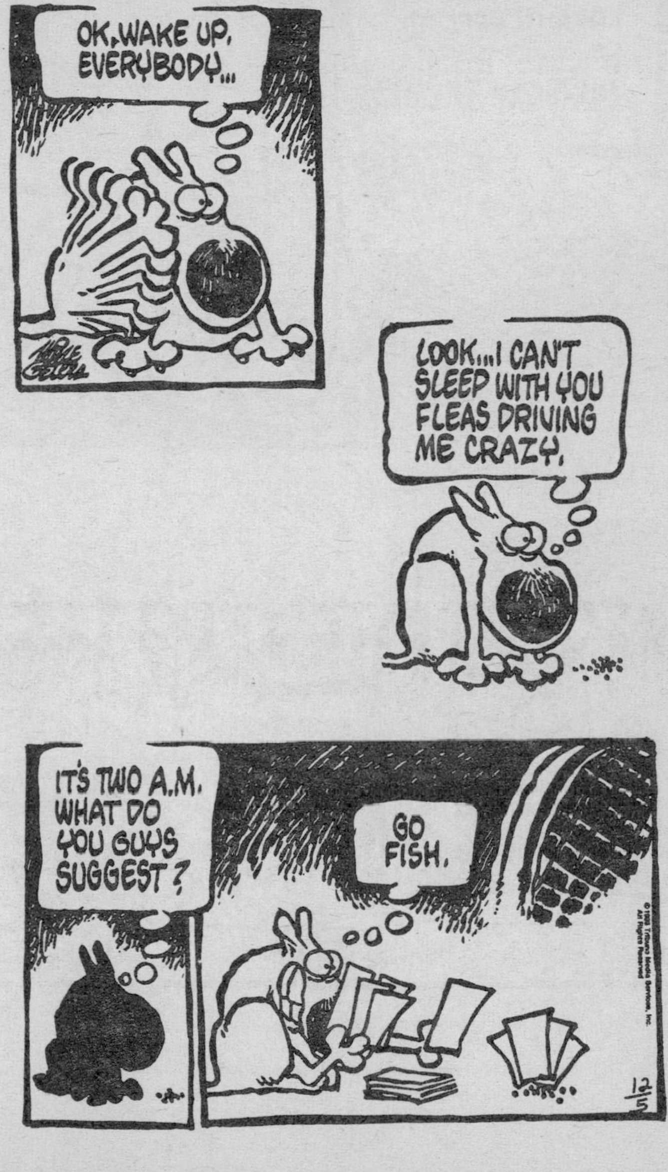
OK, WAKE UP, EVERYBODY...
LOOK...I CAN'T SLEEP WITH YOU FLEAS DRIVING ME CRAZY.
IT'S TWO A.M. WHAT DO YOU GUYS SUGGEST?
GO FISH.
12/5

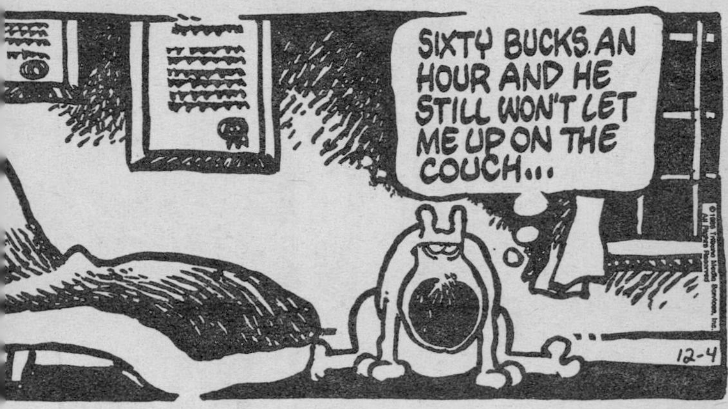
SIXTY BUCKS AN HOUR AND HE STILL WON'T LET ME UP ON THE COUCH...
12-4

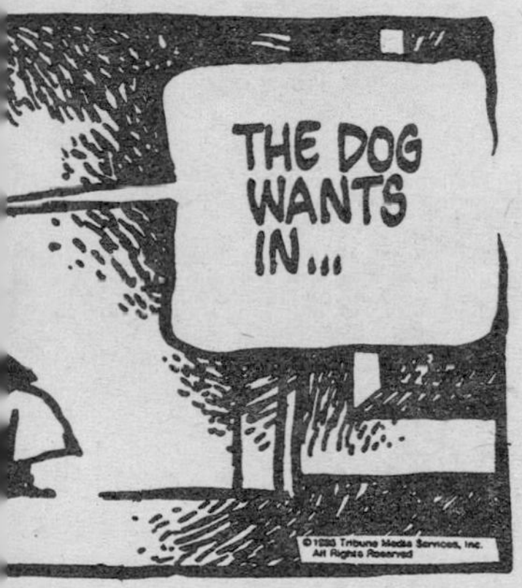
THE DOG WANTS IN...

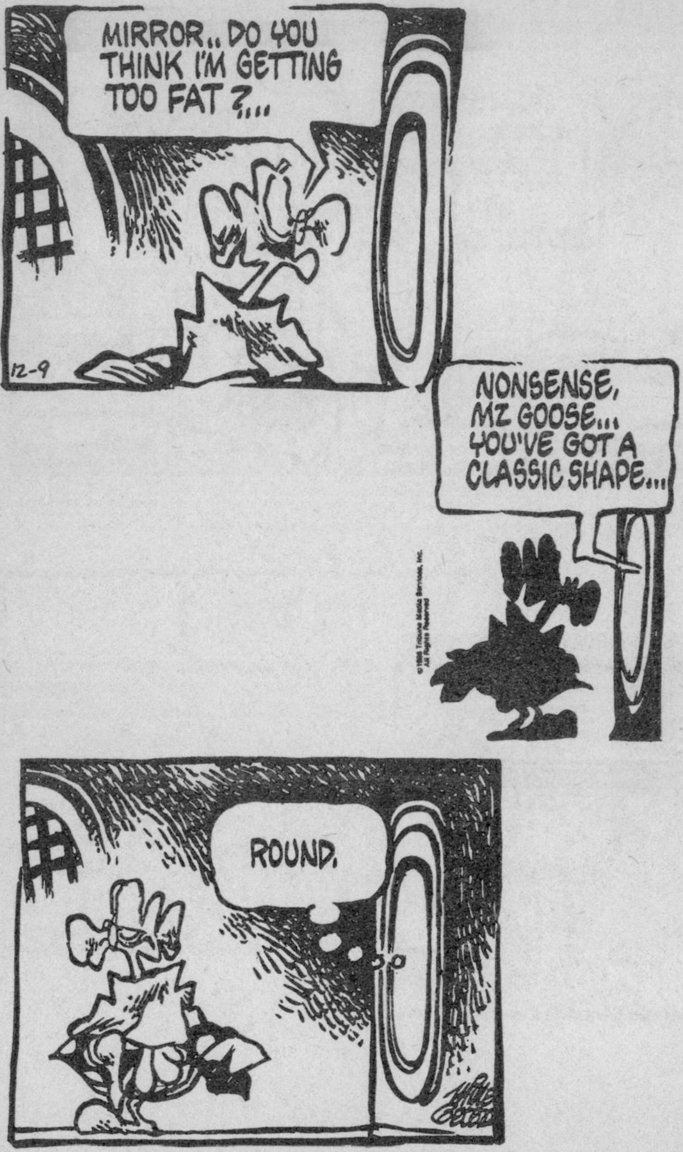
MIRROR.. DO YOU THINK I'M GETTING TOO FAT ?...
12-9
NONSENSE, MZ GOOSE... YOU'VE GOT A CLASSIC SHAPE...
ROUND.

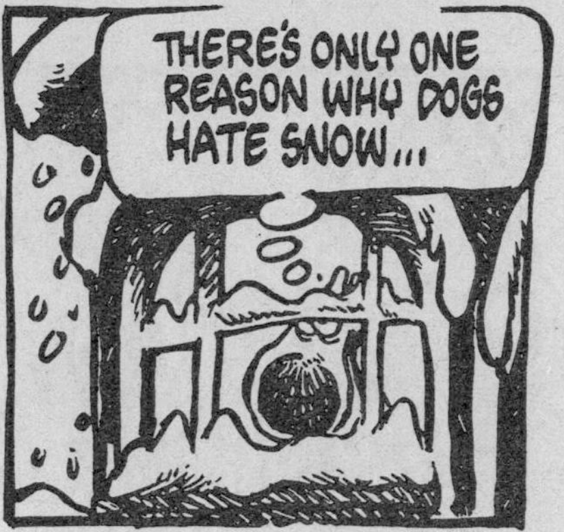
THERE'S ONLY ONE REASON WHY DOGS HATE SNOW...

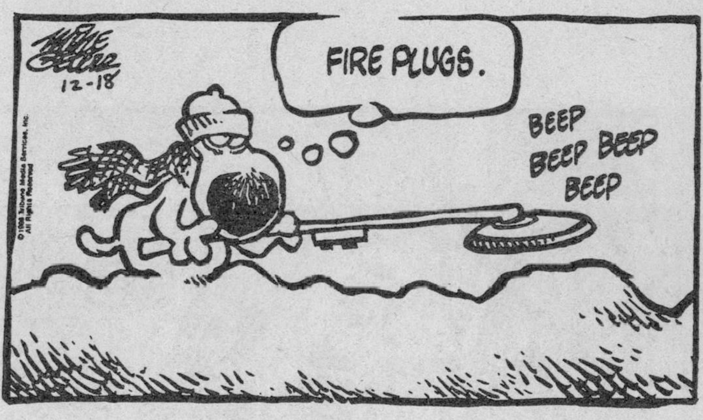
FIRE PLUGS.
BEEP
BEEP BEEP
BEEP
12-18
©1998 Tribune Media Services, Inc. All Rights Reserved

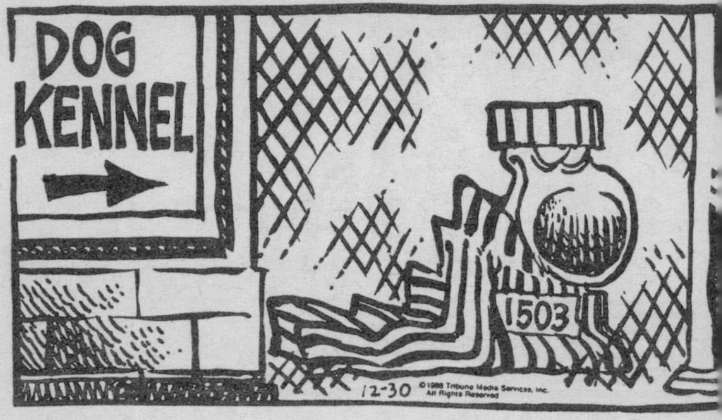
DOG
KENNEL
1503
12-30
© 1988 Tribune Media Services, Inc.
All Rights Reserved

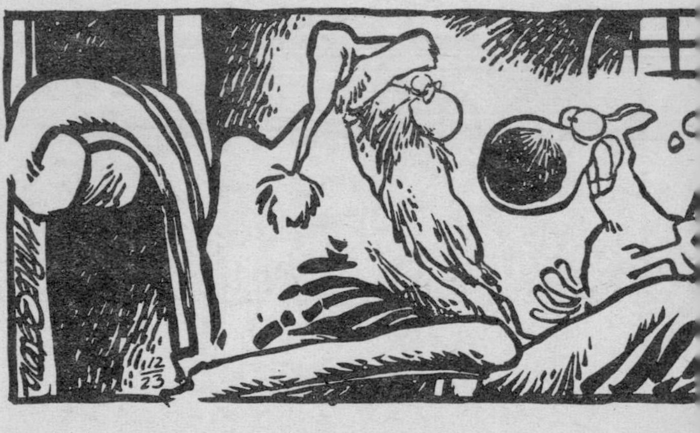
12/23

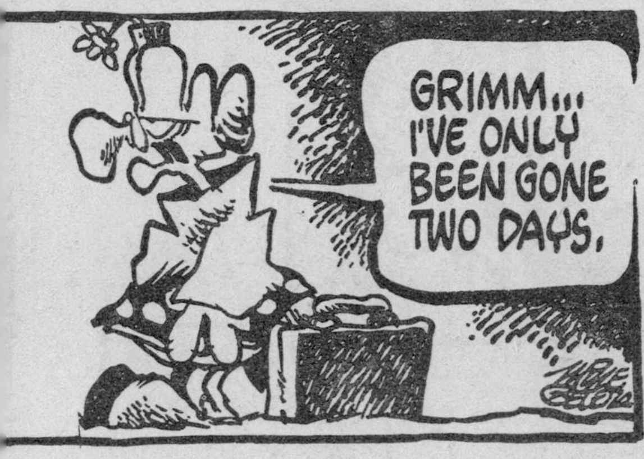
GRIMM... I'VE ONLY BEEN GONE TWO DAYS.

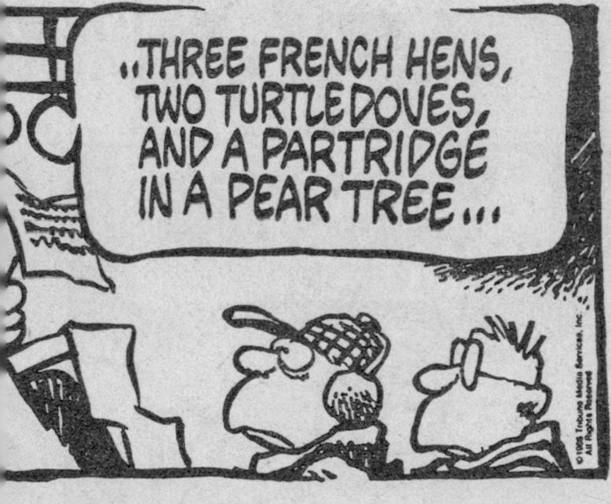
..THREE FRENCH HENS, TWO TURTLEDOVES, AND A PARTRIDGE IN A PEAR TREE...
© 1995 Tribune Media Services, Inc. All Rights Reserved

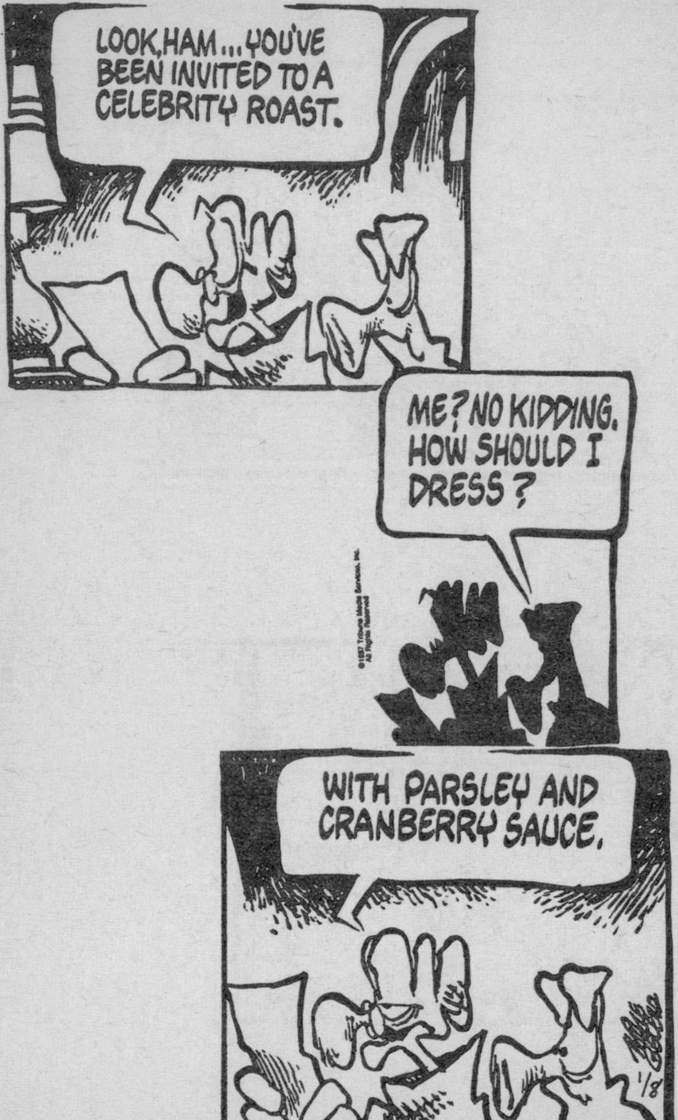
LOOK, HAM... YOU'VE BEEN INVITED TO A CELEBRITY ROAST.
ME? NO KIDDING. HOW SHOULD I DRESS?
WITH PARSLEY AND CRANBERRY SAUCE.
©1997 Tribune Media Services, Inc. All Rights Reserved
1/8

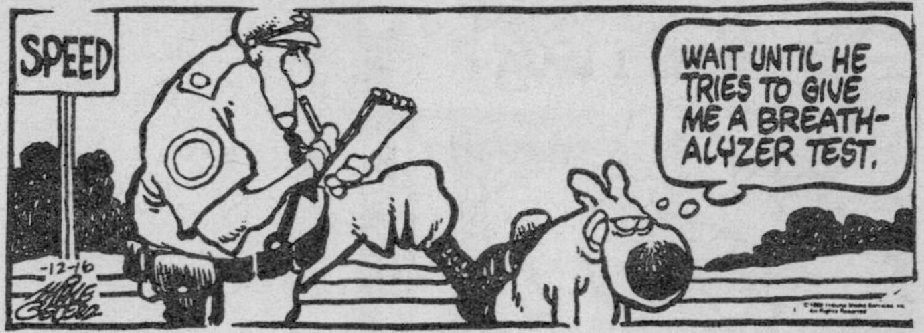
SPEED
WAIT UNTIL HE TRIES TO GIVE ME A BREATH-ALYZER TEST.

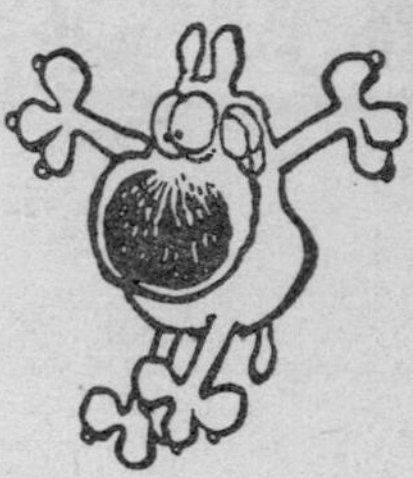

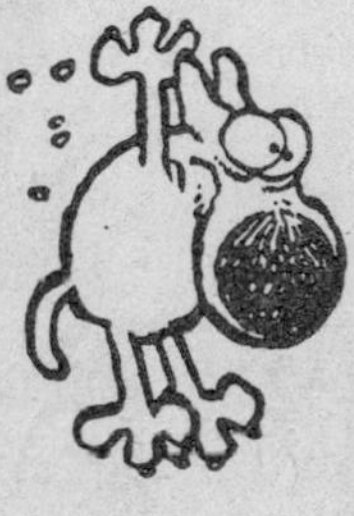

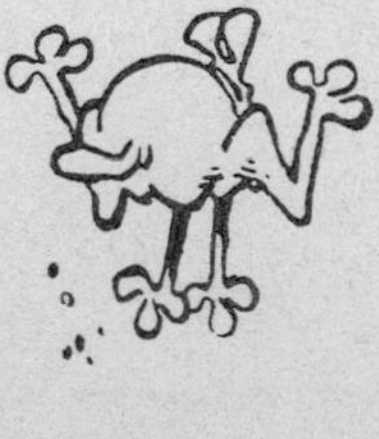

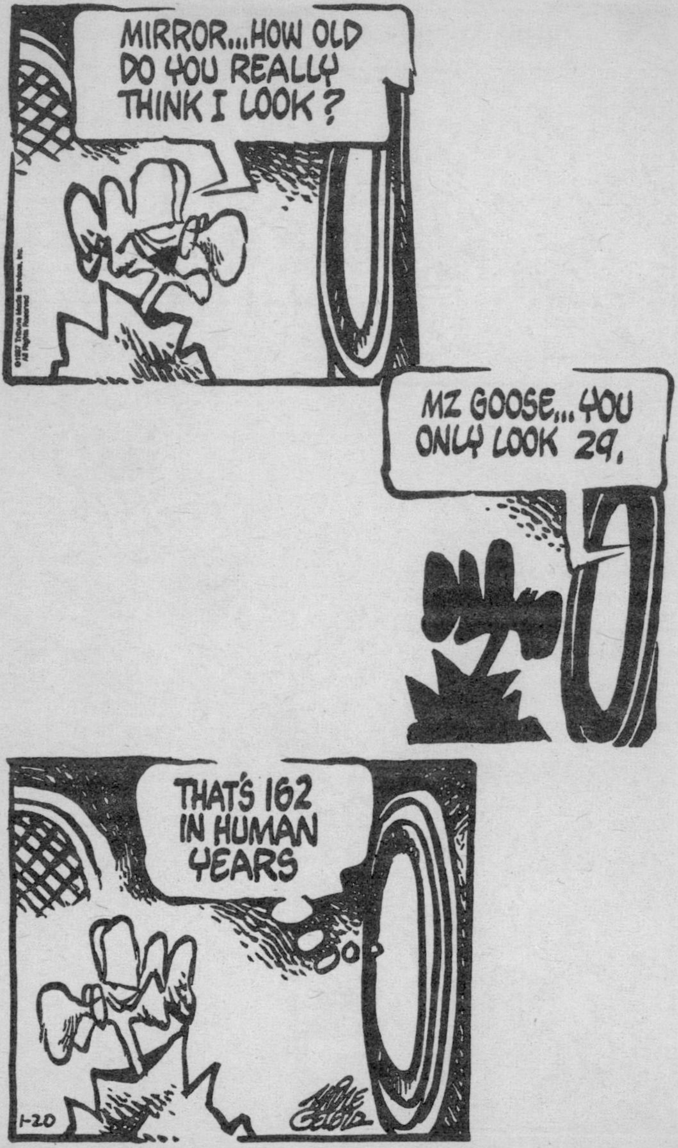
MIRROR...HOW OLD DO YOU REALLY THINK I LOOK?
©1987 Tribune Media Services, Inc.
All Rights Reserved
MZ GOOSE... YOU ONLY LOOK 29.
THAT'S 162 IN HUMAN YEARS
1-20

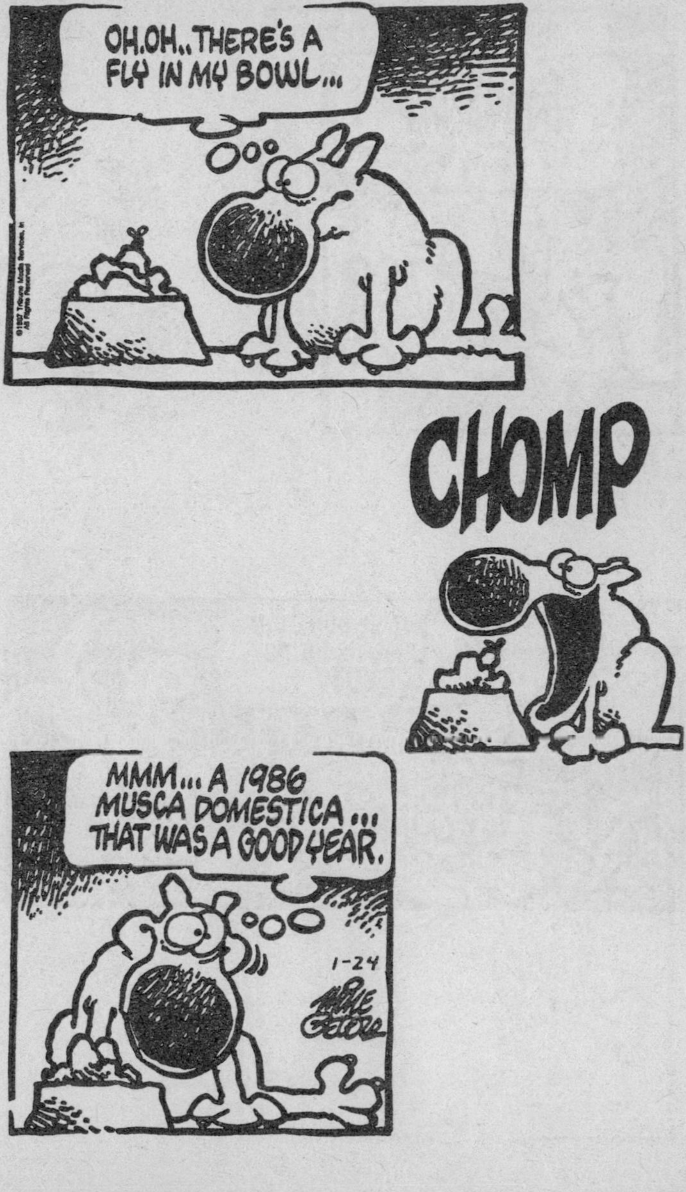
OH,OH.. THERE'S A FLY IN MY BOWL...
CHOMP
MMM... A 1986 MUSCA DOMESTICA... THAT WAS A GOOD YEAR.
1-24

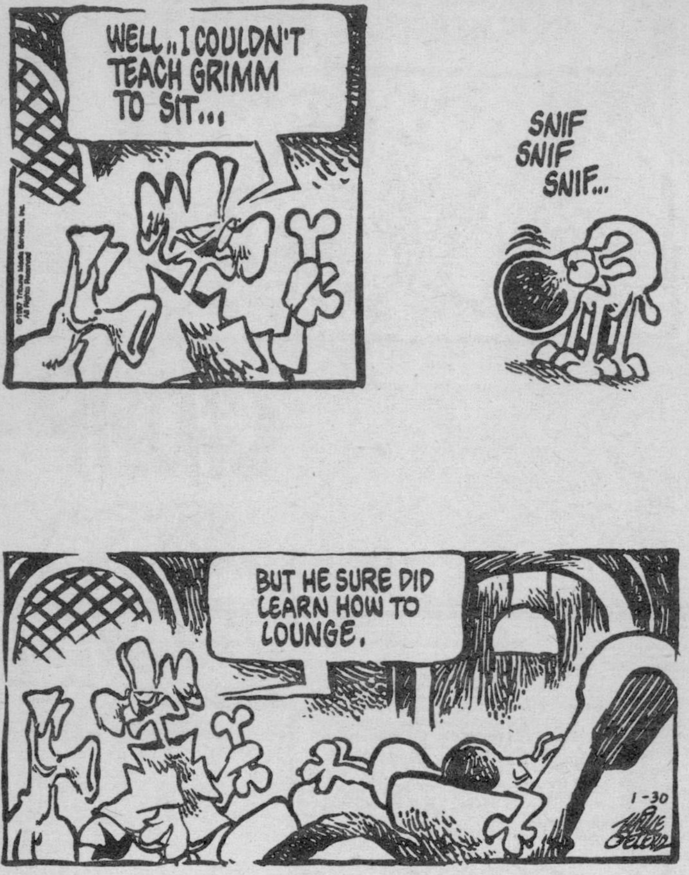

WELL.. I COULDN'T TEACH GRIMM TO SIT...
©1987 Tribune Media Services, Inc. All Rights Reserved
SNIF SNIF SNIF...
BUT HE SURE DID LEARN HOW TO LOUNGE.
1-30

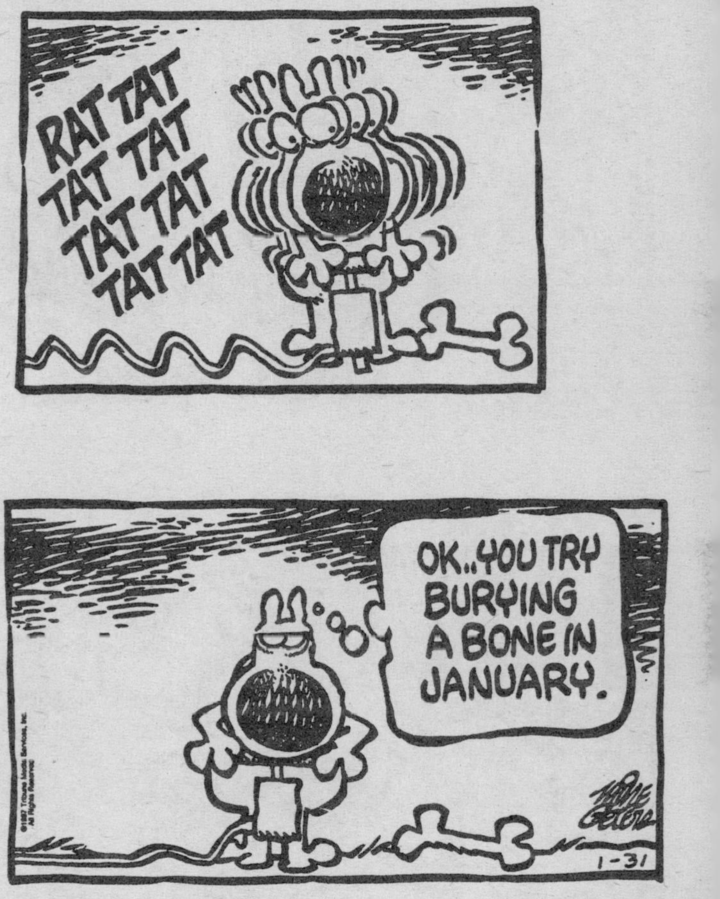
RAT TAT TAT TAT TAT TAT TAT TAT
OK..YOU TRY BURYING A BONE IN JANUARY.
©1987 Tribune Media Services, Inc.
All Rights Reserved
1-31

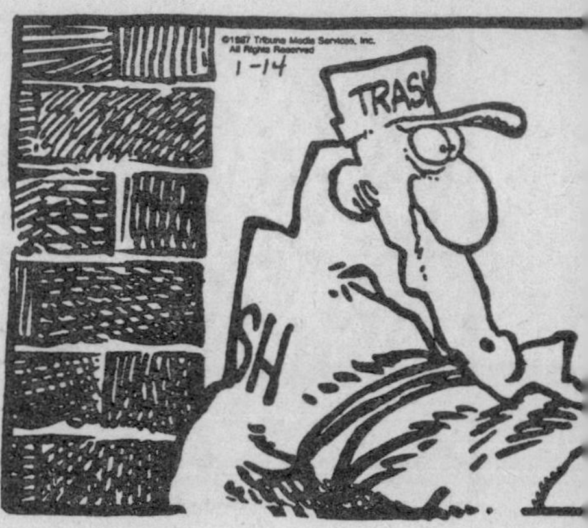
©1987 Tribune Media Services, Inc.
All Rights Reserved
1-14
TRAS
SH

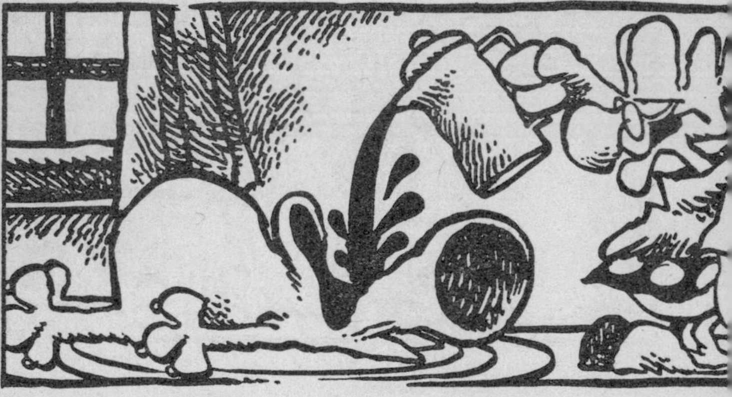

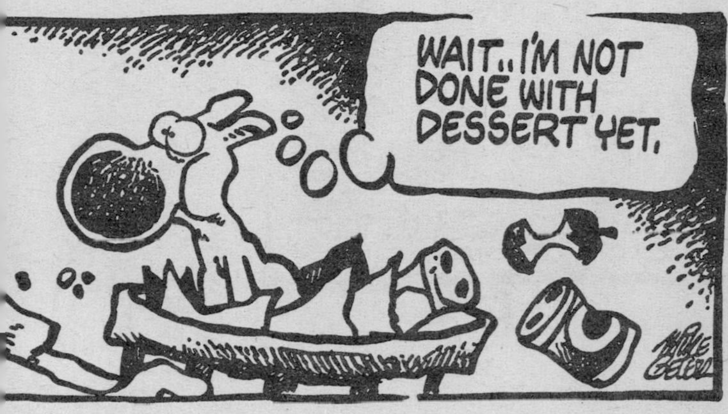
WAIT.. I'M NOT DONE WITH DESSERT YET.

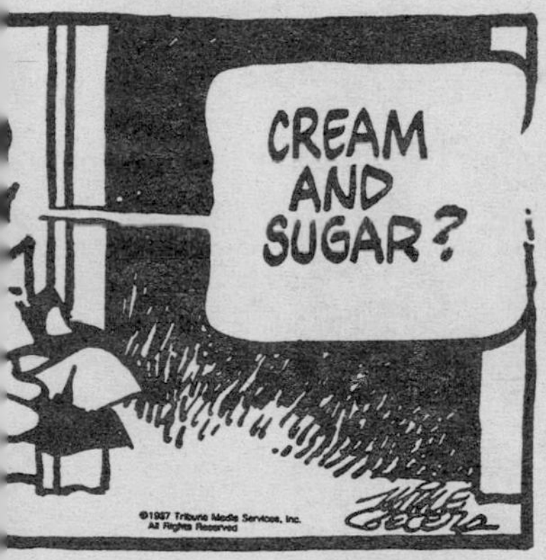
CREAM AND SUGAR?

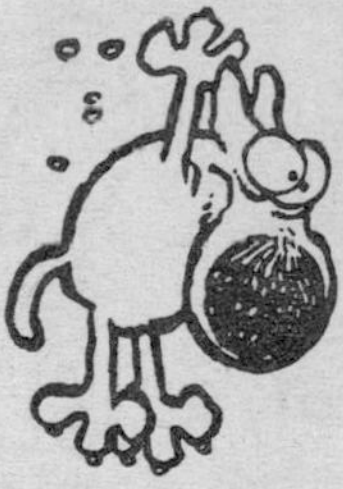

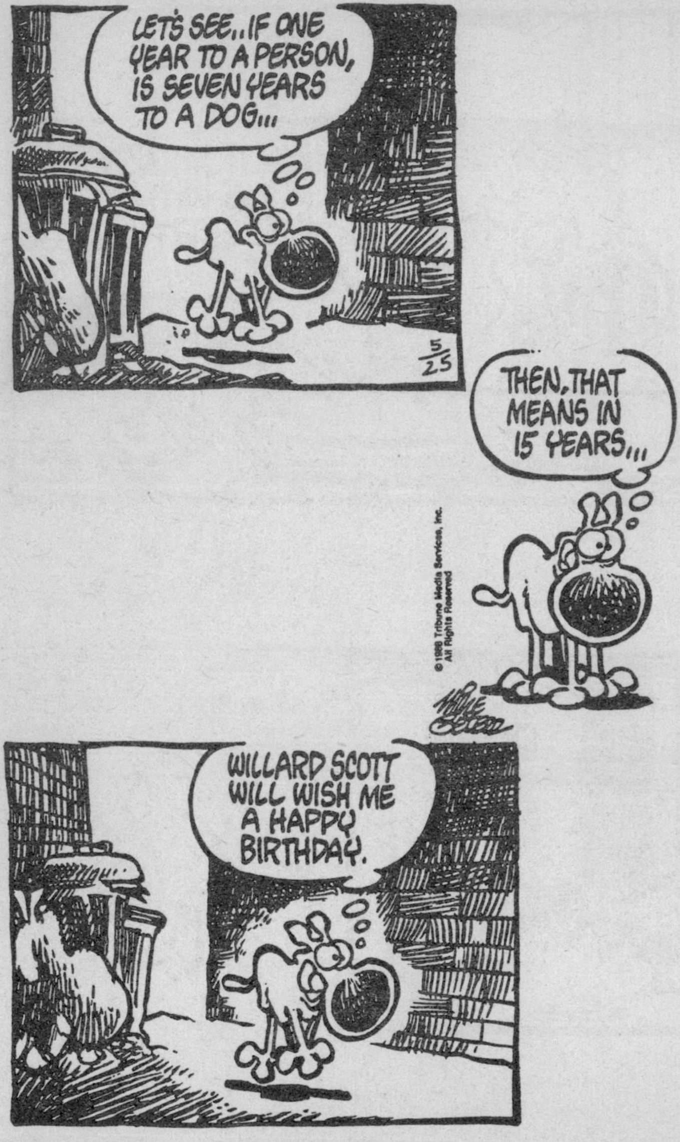
LET'S SEE..IF ONE YEAR TO A PERSON, IS SEVEN YEARS TO A DOG...
5/25
THEN, THAT MEANS IN 15 YEARS...
WILLARD SCOTT WILL WISH ME A HAPPY BIRTHDAY.

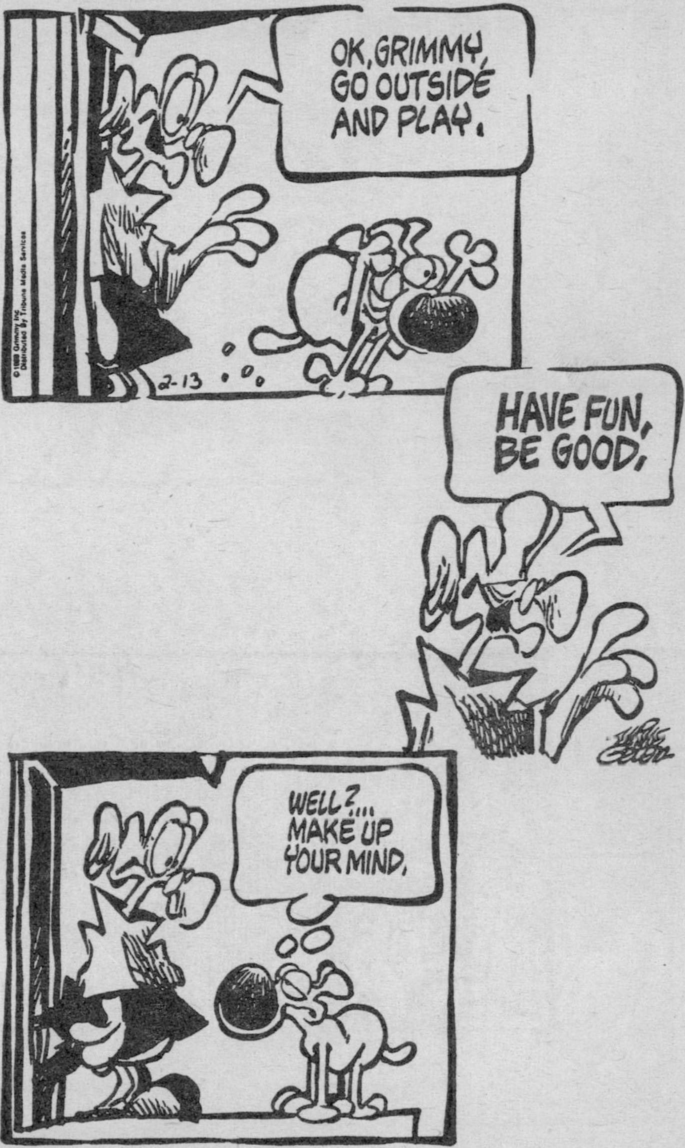
OK, GRIMMY, GO OUTSIDE AND PLAY.
Distributed By Tribune Media Services
2-13
HAVE FUN, BE GOOD,
WELL?.... MAKE UP YOUR MIND.

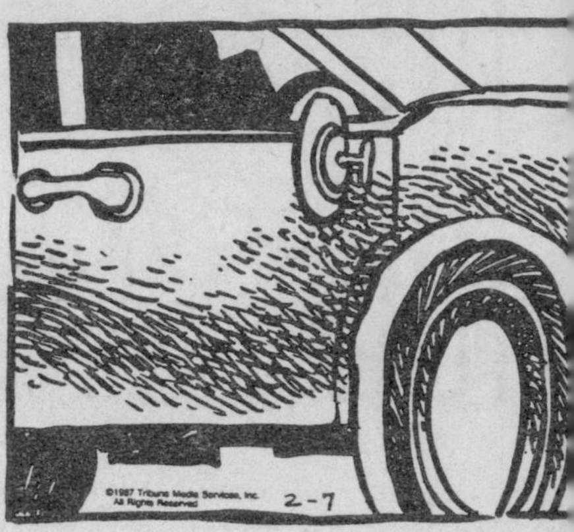
©1987 Tribune Media Services, Inc.
All Rights Reserved
2-7

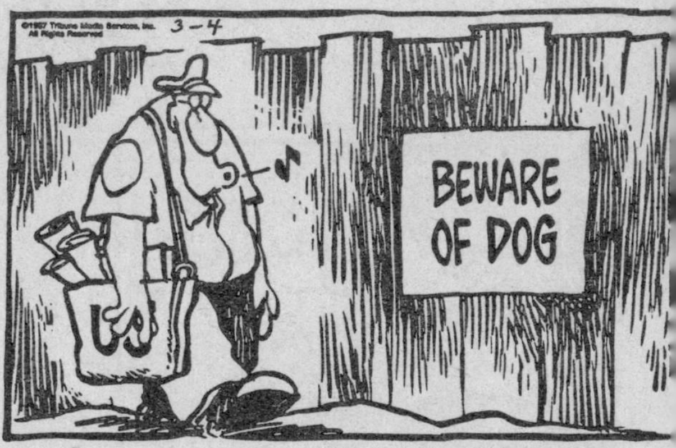
©1987 Tribune Media Services, Inc.
All Rights Reserved
3-4
BEWARE
OF DOG
US

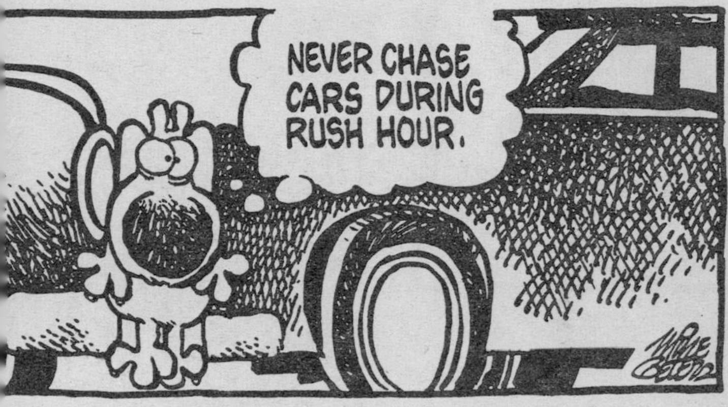
NEVER CHASE CARS DURING RUSH HOUR.

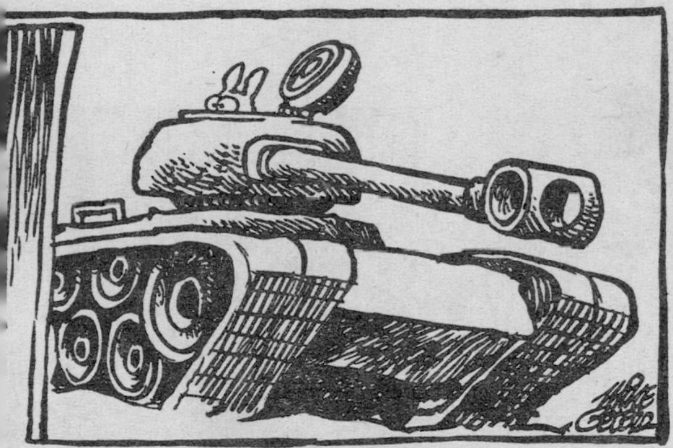

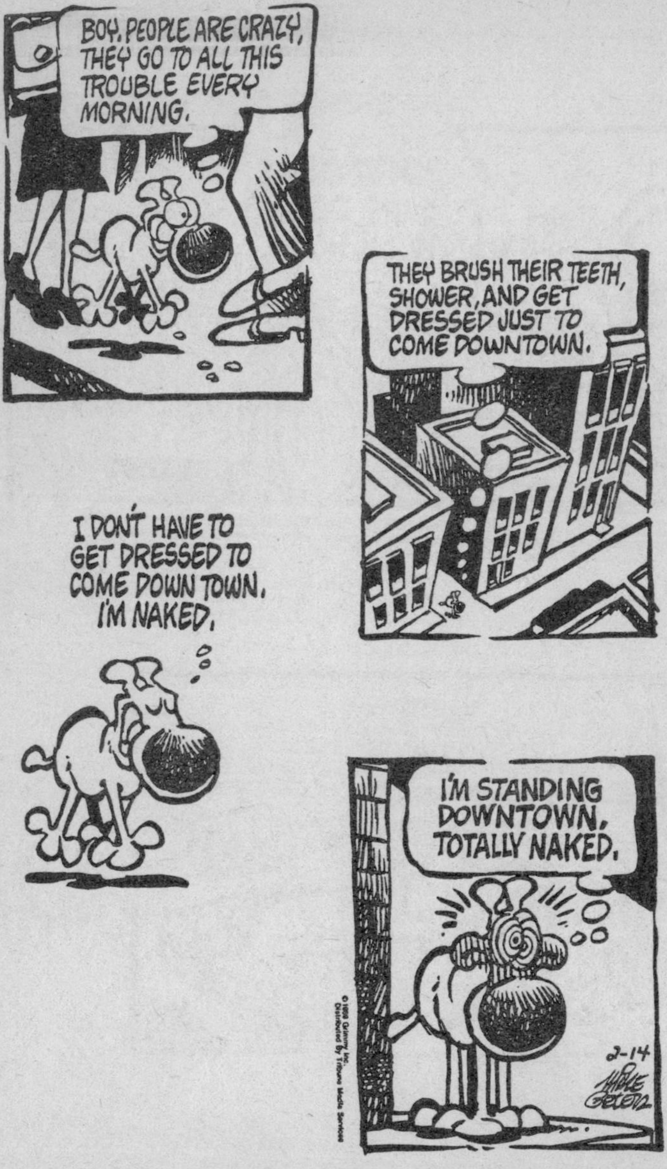
BOY, PEOPLE ARE CRAZY, THEY GO TO ALL THIS TROUBLE EVERY MORNING.
THEY BRUSH THEIR TEETH, SHOWER, AND GET DRESSED JUST TO COME DOWNTOWN.
I DON'T HAVE TO GET DRESSED TO COME DOWN TOWN. I'M NAKED.
I'M STANDING DOWNTOWN, TOTALLY NAKED.
2-14

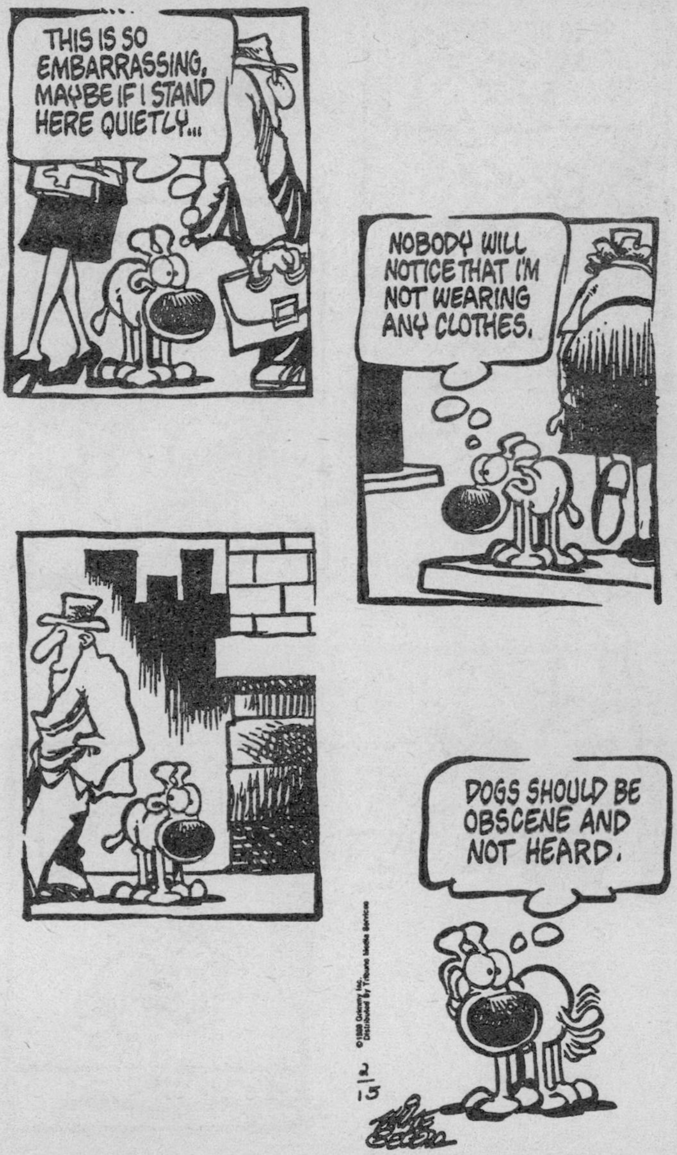

THIS IS SO EMBARRASSING, MAYBE IF I STAND HERE QUIETLY...
NOBODY WILL NOTICE THAT I'M NOT WEARING ANY CLOTHES.
DOGS SHOULD BE OBSCENE AND NOT HEARD.
Distributed by Tribune Media Services

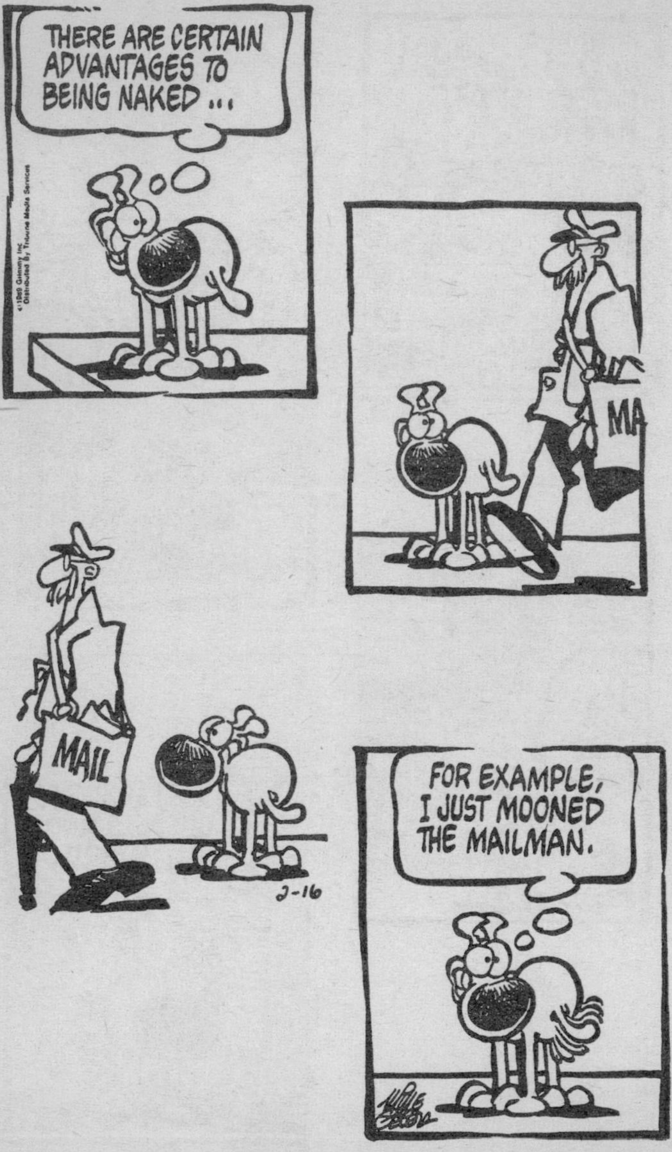
THERE ARE CERTAIN ADVANTAGES TO BEING NAKED ...
MA
MAIL
2-16
FOR EXAMPLE, I JUST MOONED THE MAILMAN.

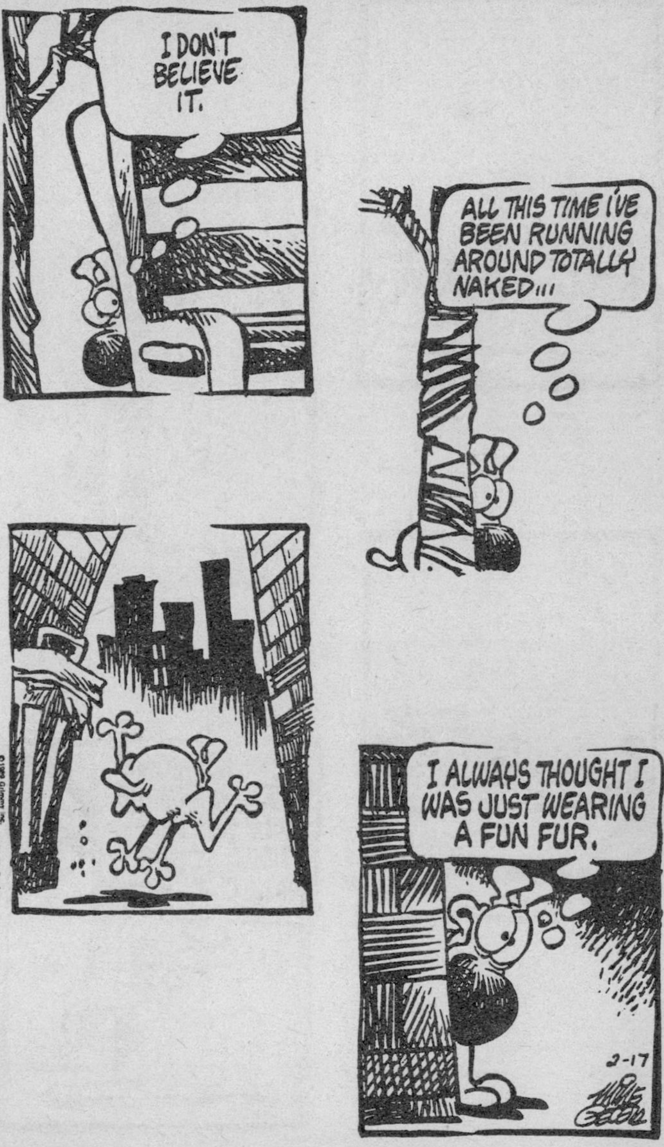
I DON'T BELIEVE IT.
ALL THIS TIME I'VE BEEN RUNNING AROUND TOTALLY NAKED...
I ALWAYS THOUGHT I WAS JUST WEARING A FUN FUR.
2-17

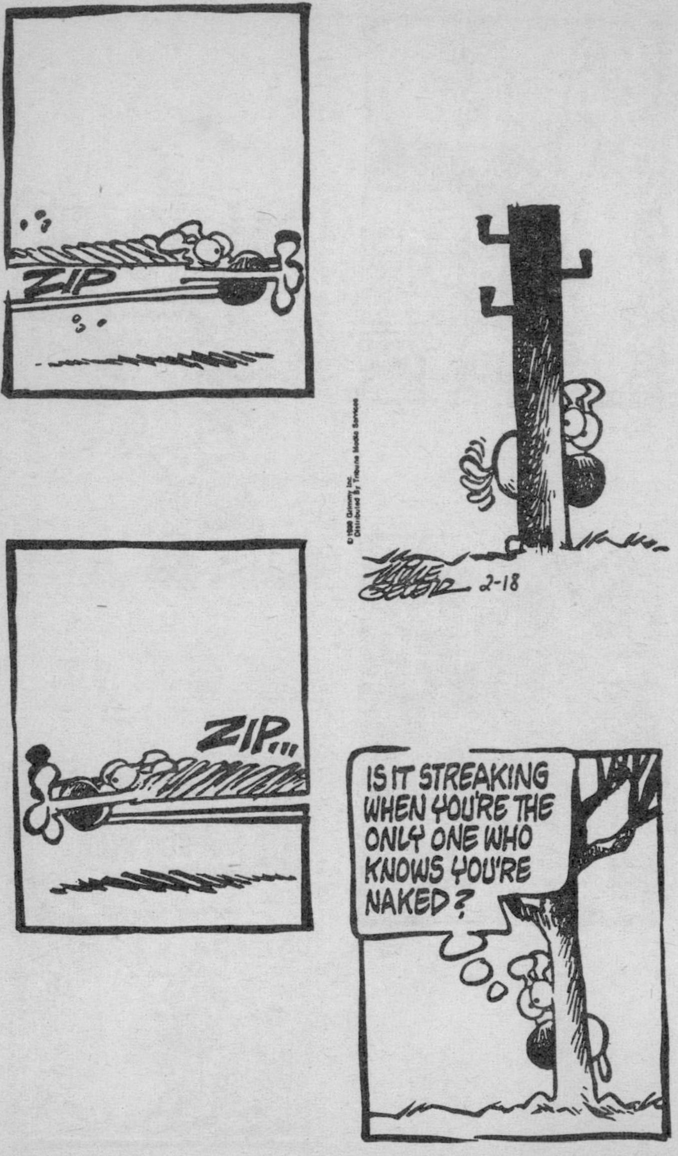
ZIP
ZIP...
2-18
Grimmy Inc.
Distributed By Tribune Media Services
IS IT STREAKING WHEN YOU'RE THE ONLY ONE WHO KNOWS YOU'RE NAKED?

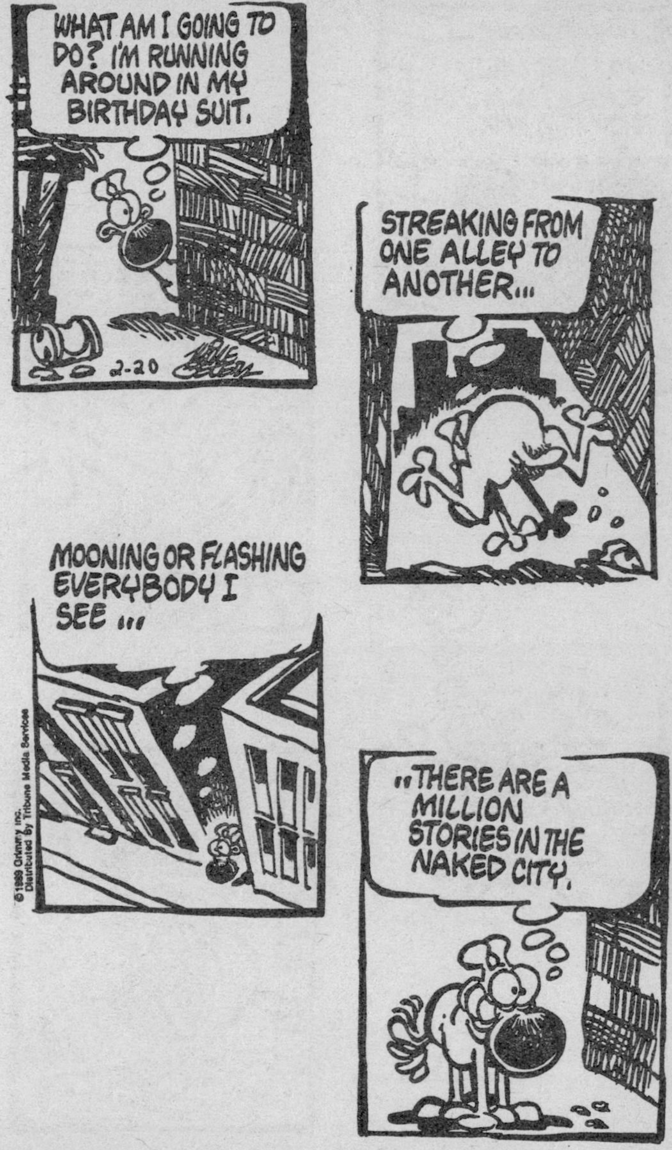

WHAT AM I GOING TO DO? I'M RUNNING AROUND IN MY BIRTHDAY SUIT.
2-20
STREAKING FROM ONE ALLEY TO ANOTHER...
MOONING OR FLASHING EVERYBODY I SEE...
...THERE ARE A MILLION STORIES IN THE NAKED CITY.

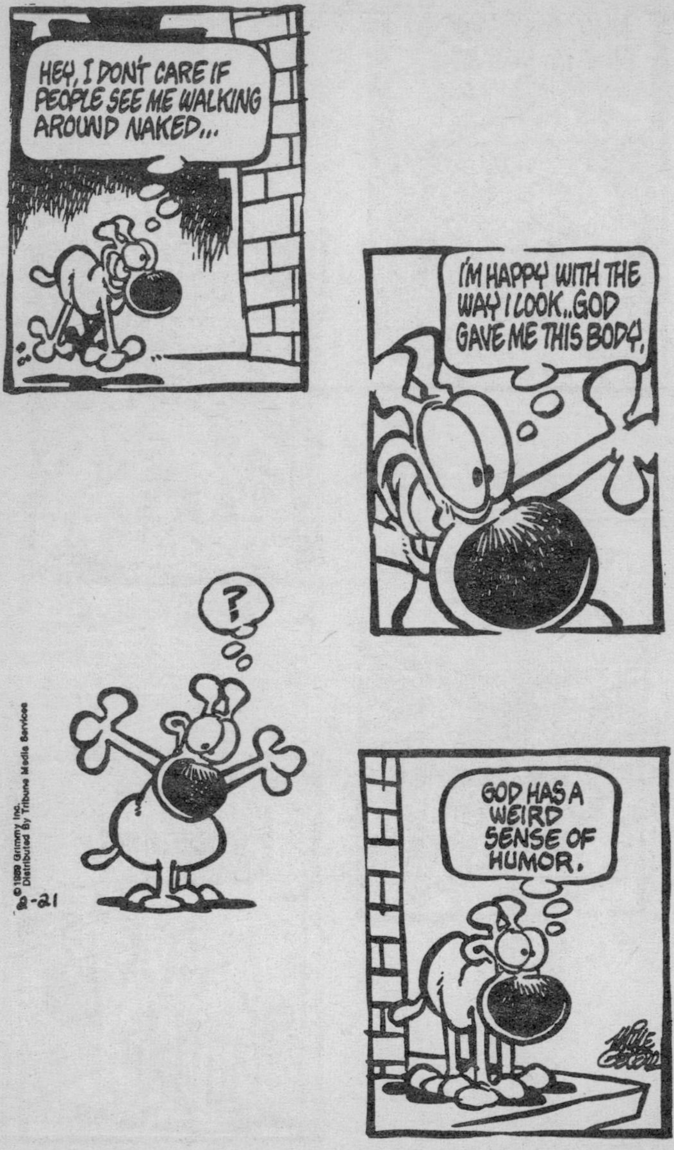
HEY, I DON'T CARE IF PEOPLE SEE ME WALKING AROUND NAKED...
I'M HAPPY WITH THE WAY I LOOK.. GOD GAVE ME THIS BODY.
?
GOD HAS A WEIRD SENSE OF HUMOR.
2-21
© 1989 Grimmy Inc.
Distributed By Tribune Media Services

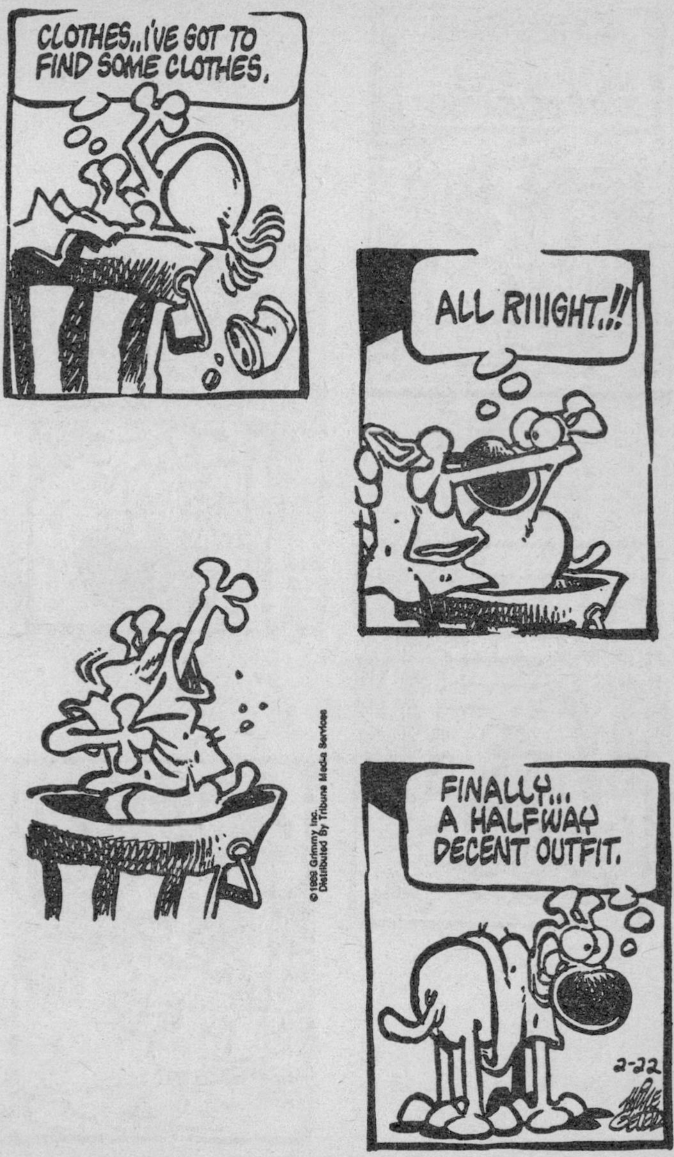
CLOTHES.. I'VE GOT TO FIND SOME CLOTHES.
ALL RIIIGHT.!!
FINALLY... A HALFWAY DECENT OUTFIT.
2-22
© 1988 Grimmy Inc.
Distributed By Tribune Media Services

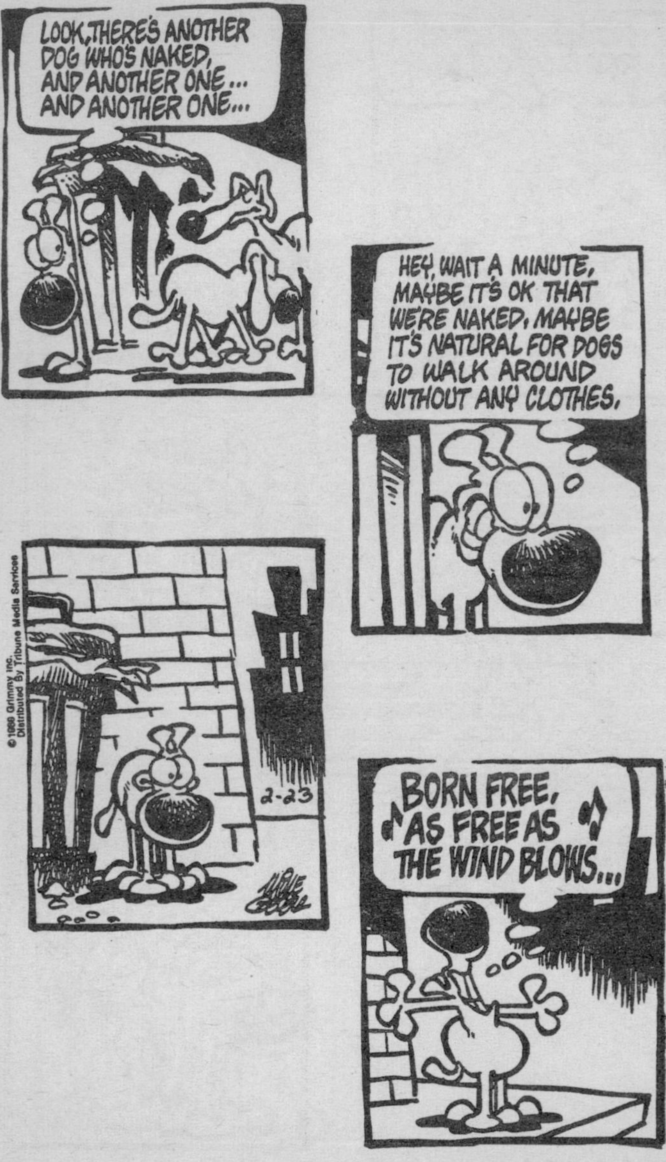
LOOK, THERE'S ANOTHER DOG WHO'S NAKED, AND ANOTHER ONE... AND ANOTHER ONE...
HEY, WAIT A MINUTE, MAYBE IT'S OK THAT WE'RE NAKED. MAYBE IT'S NATURAL FOR DOGS TO WALK AROUND WITHOUT ANY CLOTHES.
2-23
BORN FREE, AS FREE AS THE WIND BLOWS...
© 1988 Grimmy Inc.
Distributed By Tribune Media Services

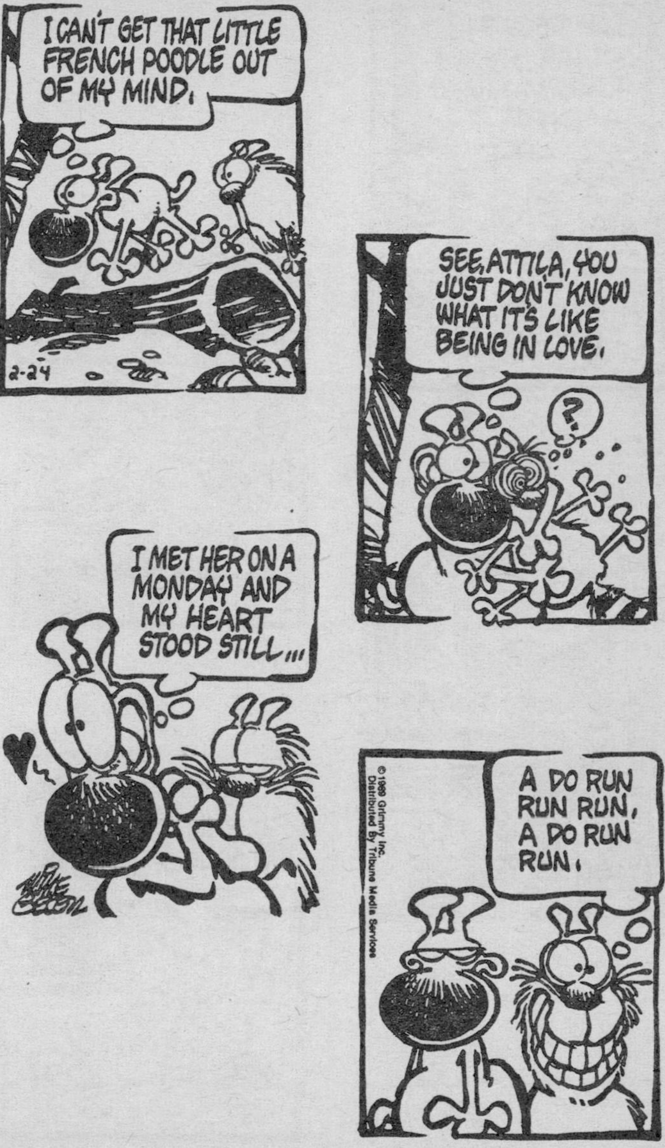
I CAN'T GET THAT LITTLE FRENCH POODLE OUT OF MY MIND.
2-24
SEE, ATTILA, YOU JUST DON'T KNOW WHAT IT'S LIKE BEING IN LOVE.
?
I MET HER ON A MONDAY AND MY HEART STOOD STILL...
A DO RUN RUN RUN, A DO RUN RUN.
© 1989 Grimmy Inc.
Distributed By Tribune Media Services

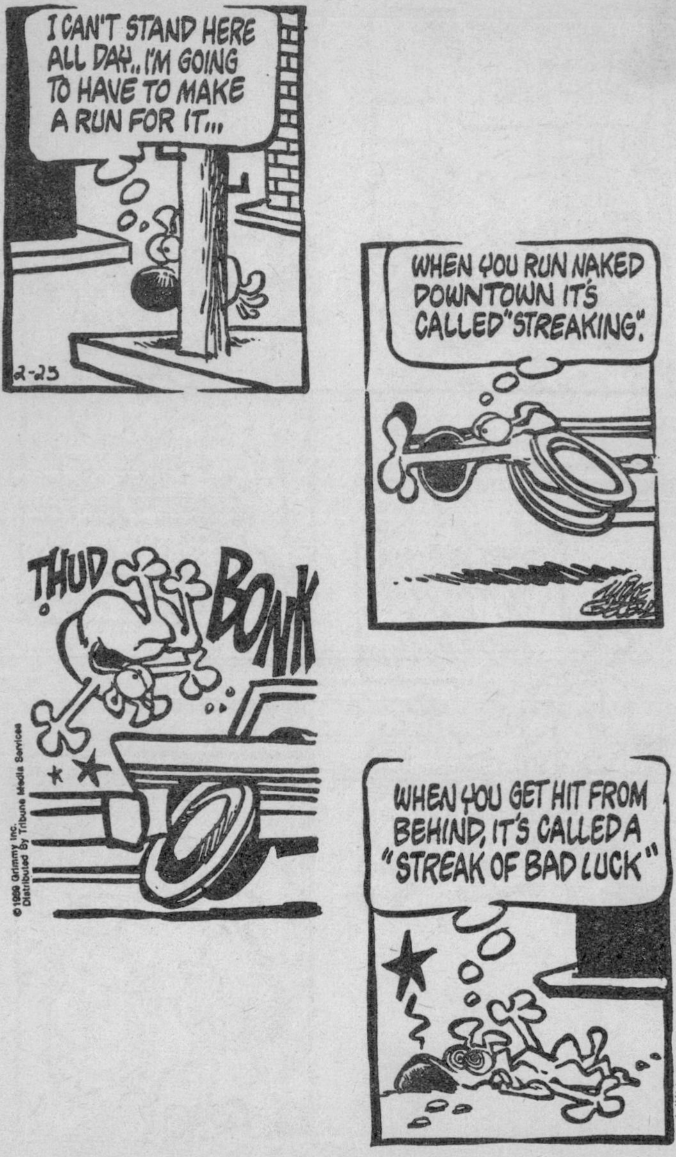
I CAN'T STAND HERE ALL DAY.. I'M GOING TO HAVE TO MAKE A RUN FOR IT...
2-25
WHEN YOU RUN NAKED DOWNTOWN IT'S CALLED "STREAKING".
THUD
BONK
© 1988 Grimmy Inc.
Distributed By Tribune Media Services
WHEN YOU GET HIT FROM BEHIND, IT'S CALLED A "STREAK OF BAD LUCK"

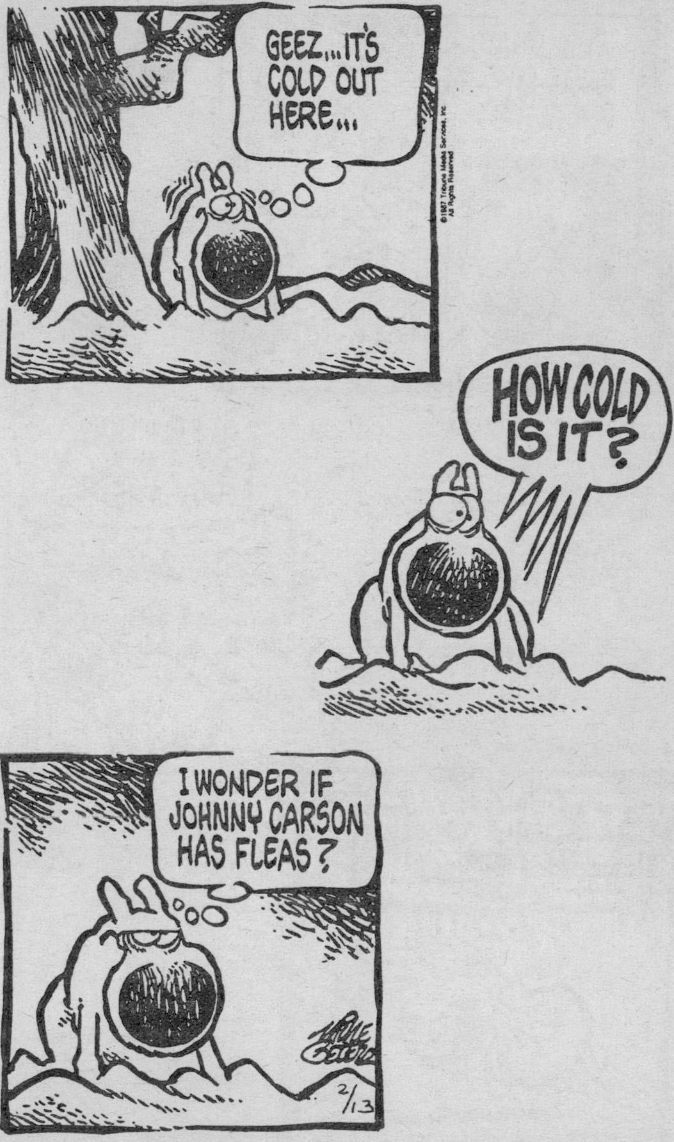
GEEZ...IT'S COLD OUT HERE...
©1987 Tribune Media Services, Inc
All Rights Reserved
HOW COLD IS IT?
I WONDER IF JOHNNY CARSON HAS FLEAS?
2/13

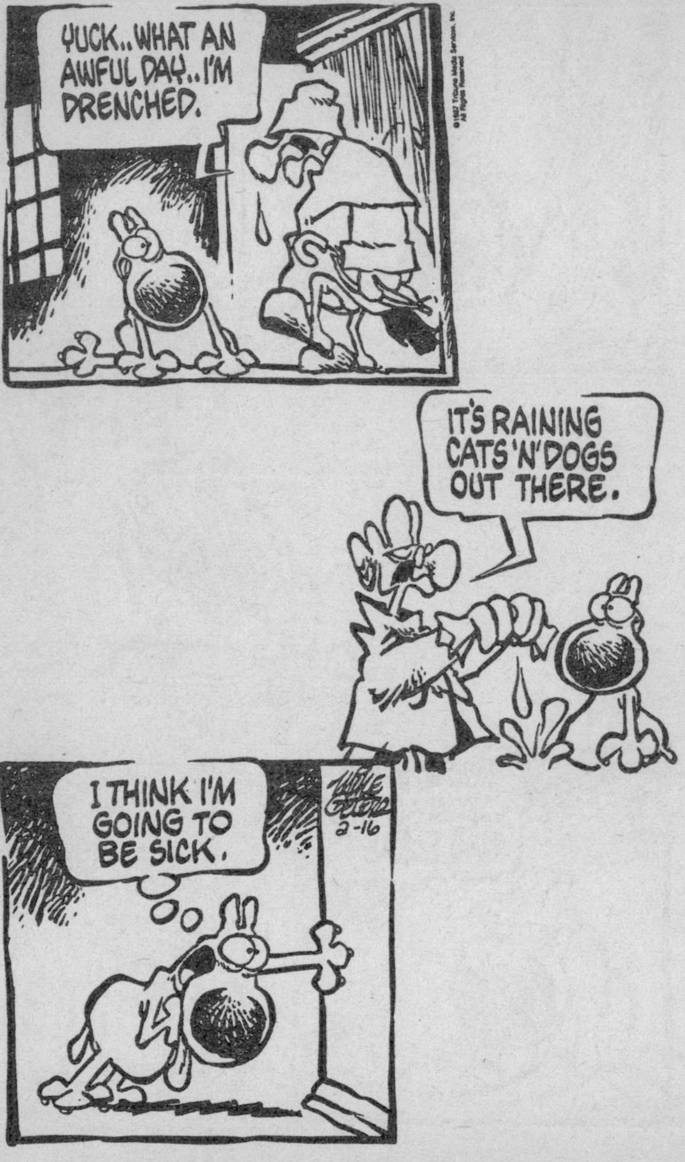
YUCK.. WHAT AN AWFUL DAY.. I'M DRENCHED.
©1987 Tribune Media Services, Inc. All Rights Reserved
IT'S RAINING CATS 'N' DOGS OUT THERE.
I THINK I'M GOING TO BE SICK.
2-16

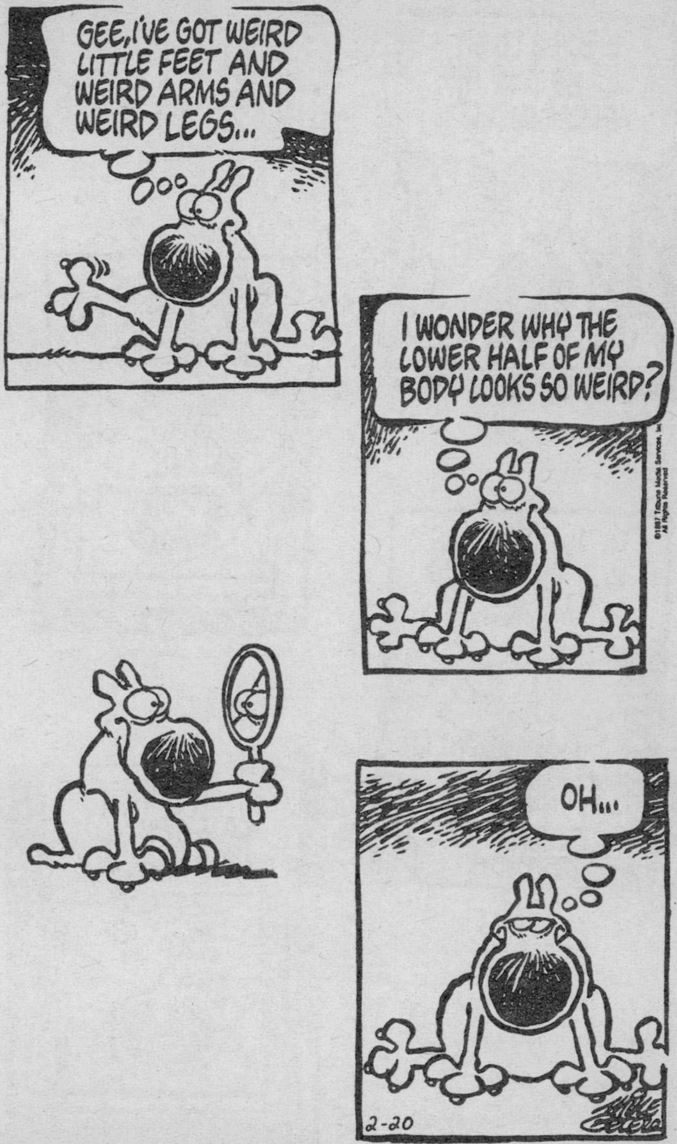
GEE, I'VE GOT WEIRD LITTLE FEET AND WEIRD ARMS AND WEIRD LEGS...
I WONDER WHY THE LOWER HALF OF MY BODY LOOKS SO WEIRD?
©1987 Tribune Media Services, Inc. All Rights Reserved
OH...
2-20

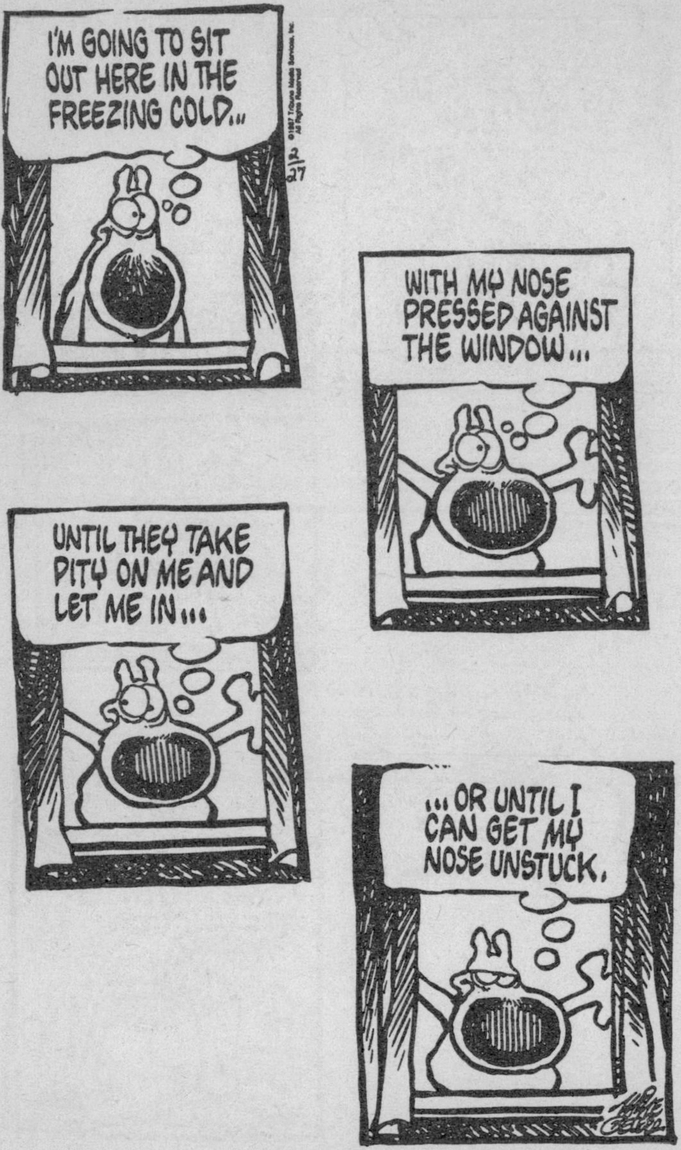
I'M GOING TO SIT OUT HERE IN THE FREEZING COLD...
WITH MY NOSE PRESSED AGAINST THE WINDOW...
UNTIL THEY TAKE PITY ON ME AND LET ME IN...
...OR UNTIL I CAN GET MY NOSE UNSTUCK.

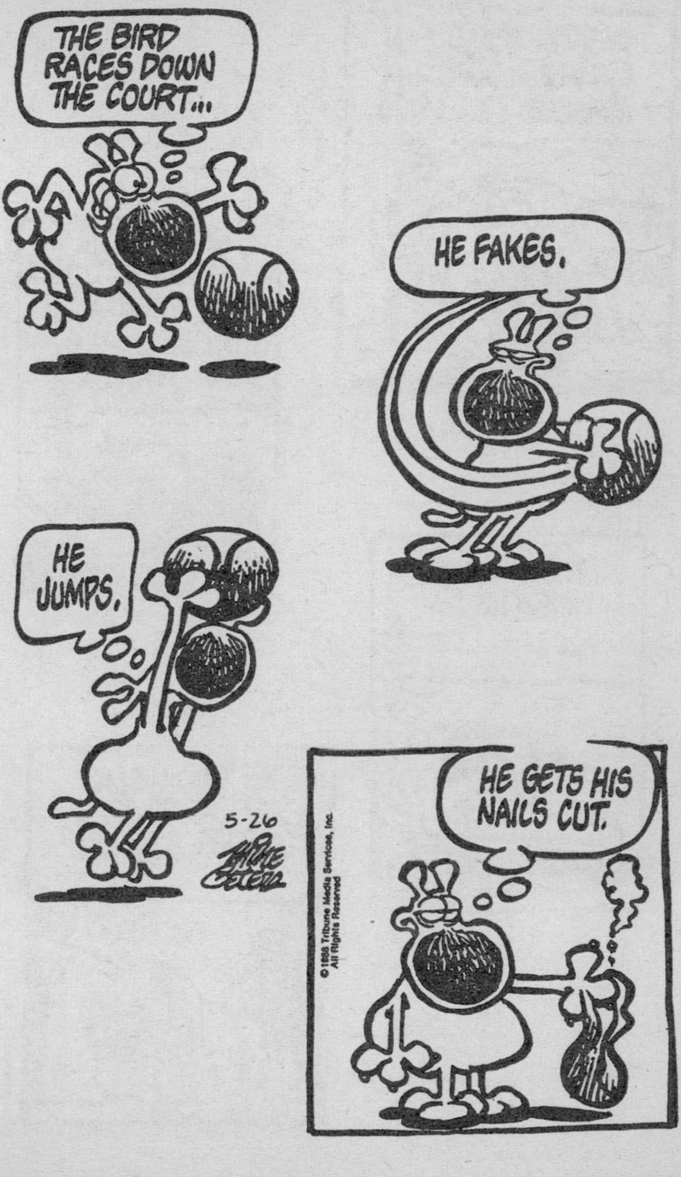
THE BIRD RACES DOWN THE COURT...
HE FAKES.
HE JUMPS.
5-26
HE GETS HIS NAILS CUT.
© 1988 Tribune Media Services, Inc.
All Rights Reserved

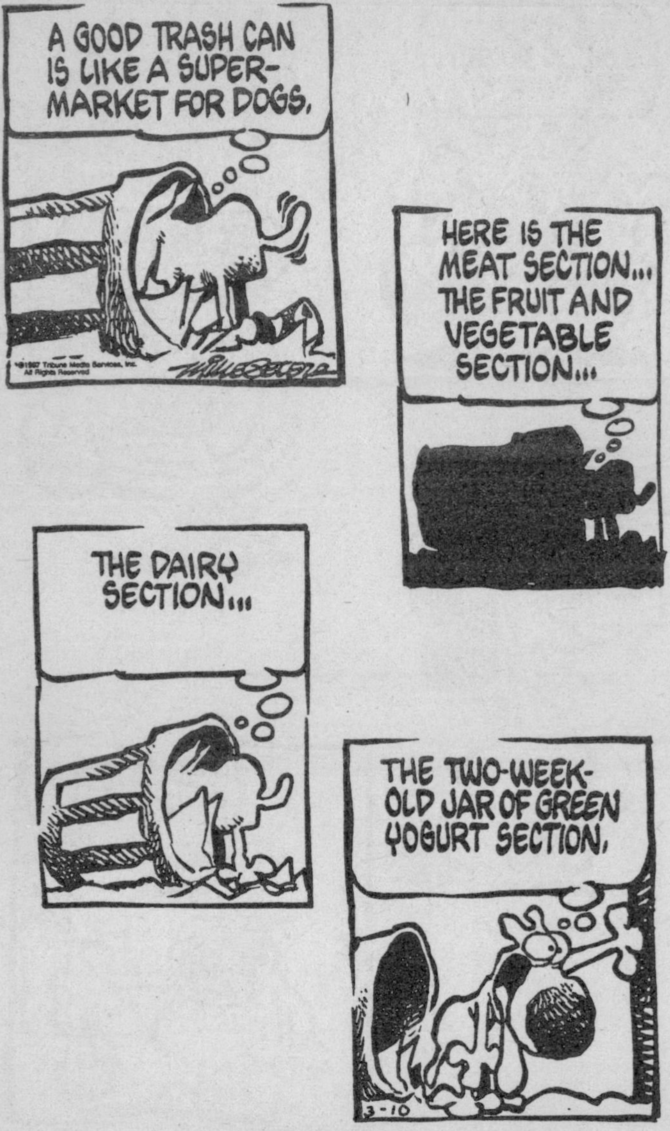
A GOOD TRASH CAN IS LIKE A SUPER-MARKET FOR DOGS.
©1987 Tribune Media Services, Inc. All Rights Reserved
HERE IS THE MEAT SECTION... THE FRUIT AND VEGETABLE SECTION...
THE DAIRY SECTION...
THE TWO-WEEK-OLD JAR OF GREEN YOGURT SECTION.
3-10

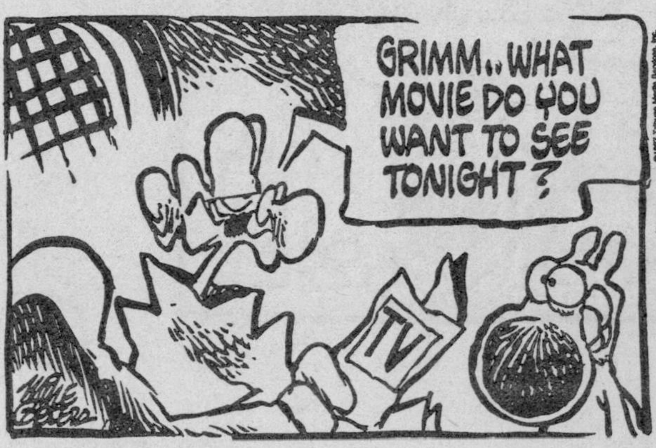
GRIMM.. WHAT MOVIE DO YOU WANT TO SEE TONIGHT?
©1997 Tribune Media Services, Inc.
All Rights Reserved
MIKE PETERS

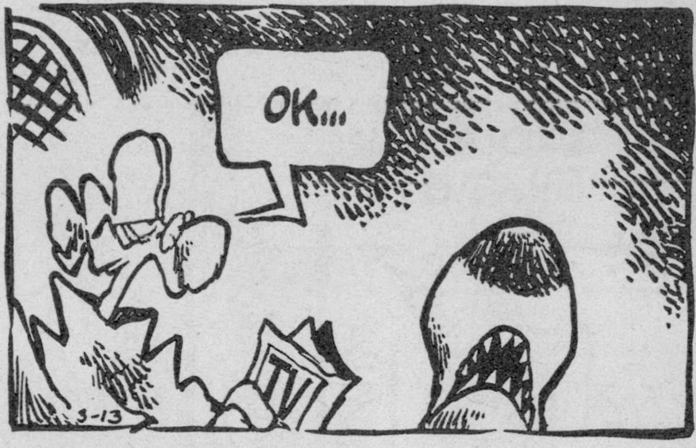
OK...
3-13

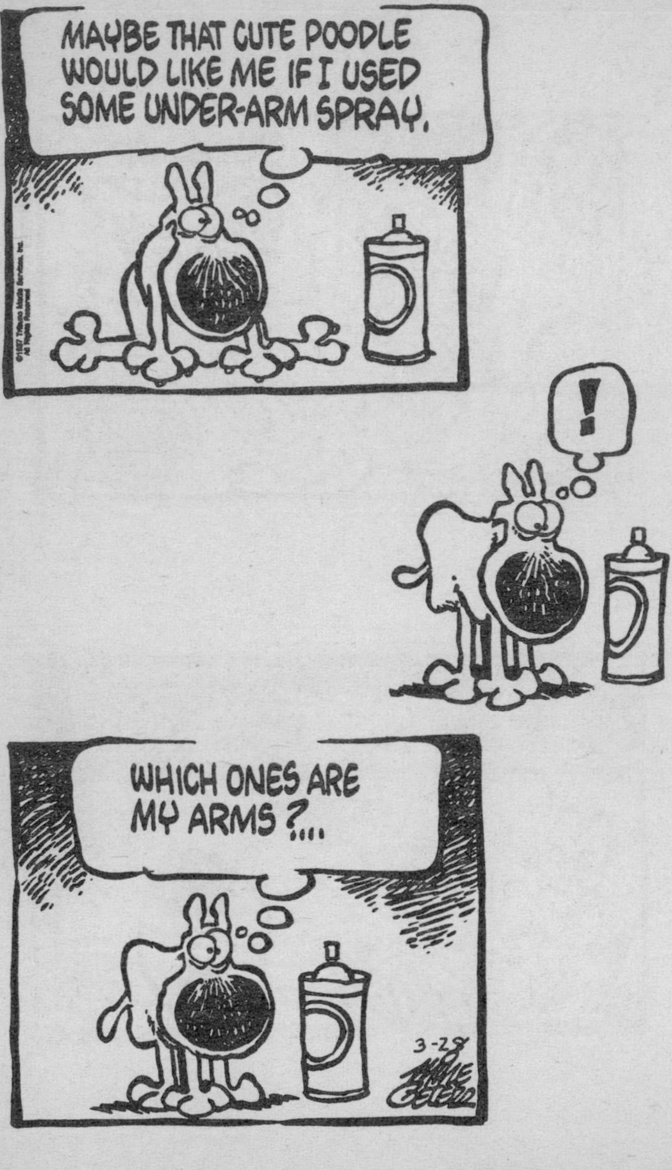
MAYBE THAT CUTE POODLE WOULD LIKE ME IF I USED SOME UNDER-ARM SPRAY.
©1987 Tribune Media Services, Inc. All Rights Reserved
!
WHICH ONES ARE MY ARMS ?....
3-28

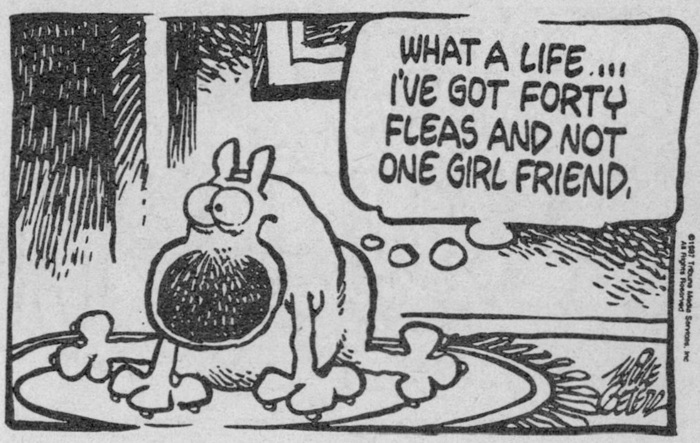
WHAT A LIFE.... I'VE GOT FORTY FLEAS AND NOT ONE GIRL FRIEND.
©1987 Tribune Media Services, Inc All Rights Reserved
MIKE PETERS

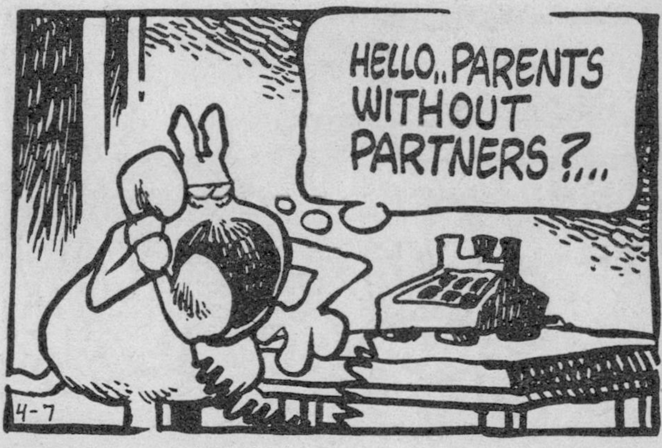
HELLO.. PARENTS WITHOUT PARTNERS ?...
4-7

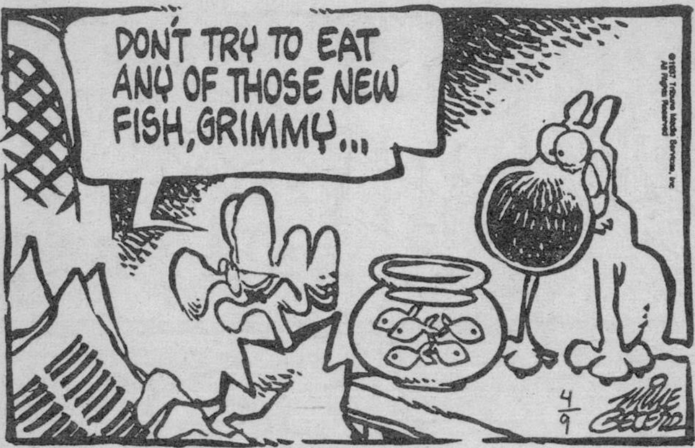
DON'T TRY TO EAT ANY OF THOSE NEW FISH, GRIMMY...
Tribune Media Services, Inc
All Rights Reserved
4/9

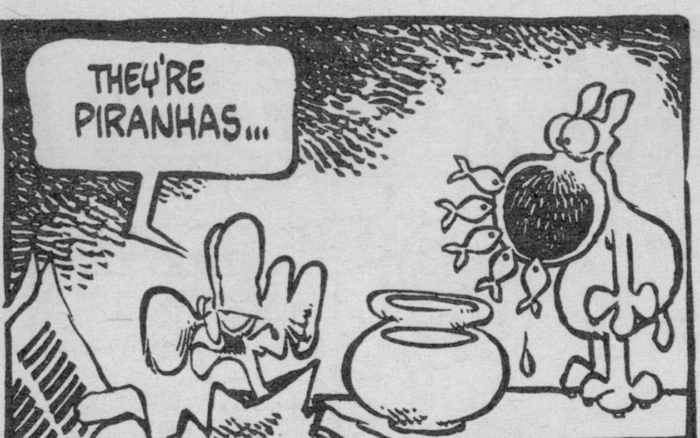
THEY'RE PIRANHAS...

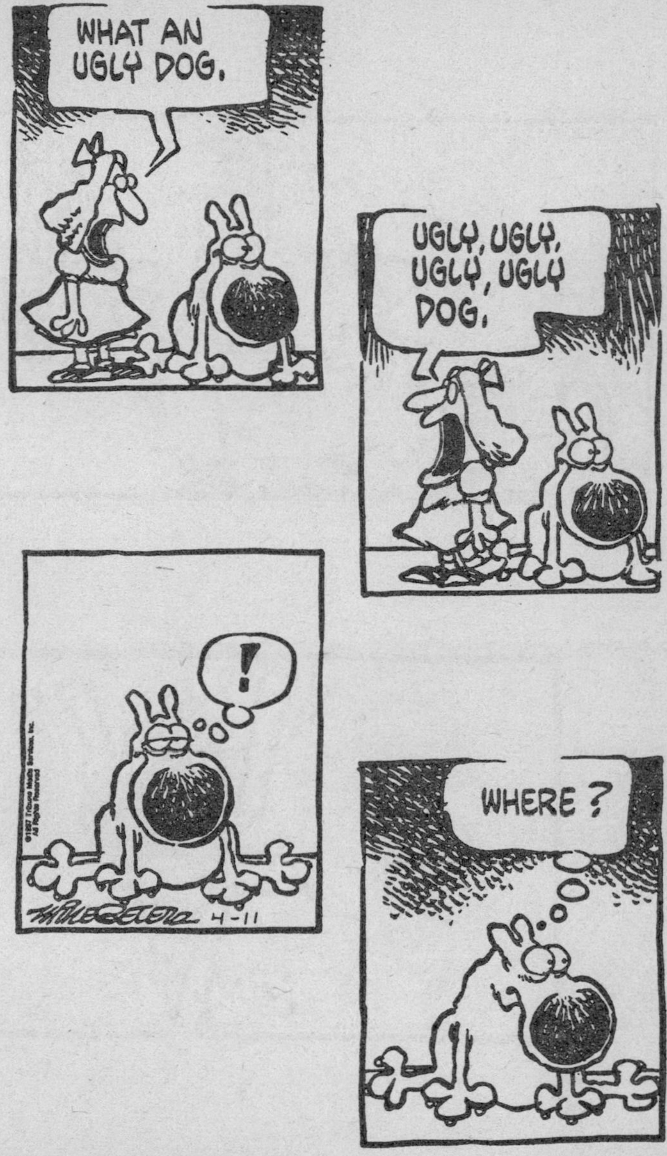
WHAT AN UGLY DOG.
UGLY, UGLY, UGLY, UGLY DOG.
!
WHERE ?
4-11

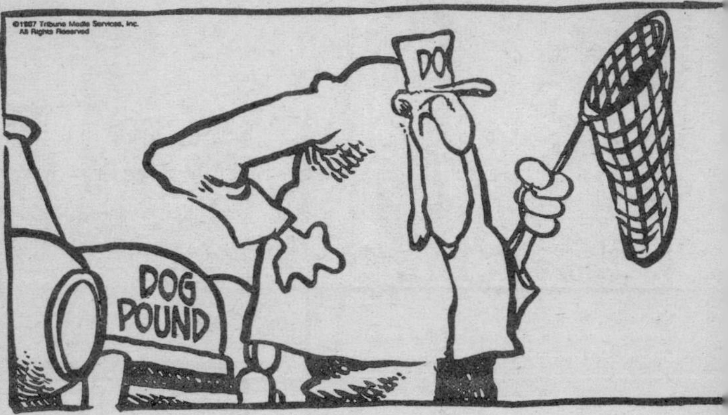
©1987 Tribune Media Services, Inc.
All Rights Reserved
DO
DOG
POUND

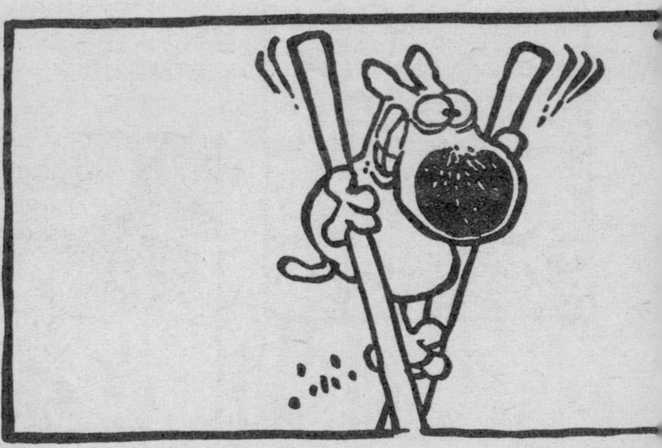

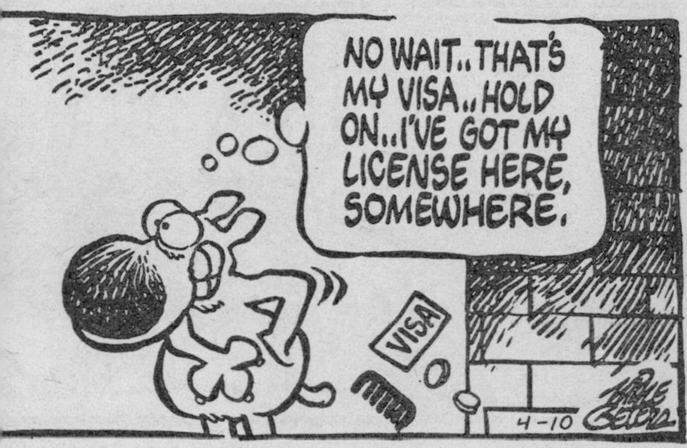
NO WAIT.. THAT'S MY VISA.. HOLD ON.. I'VE GOT MY LICENSE HERE, SOMEWHERE.
VISA
4-10

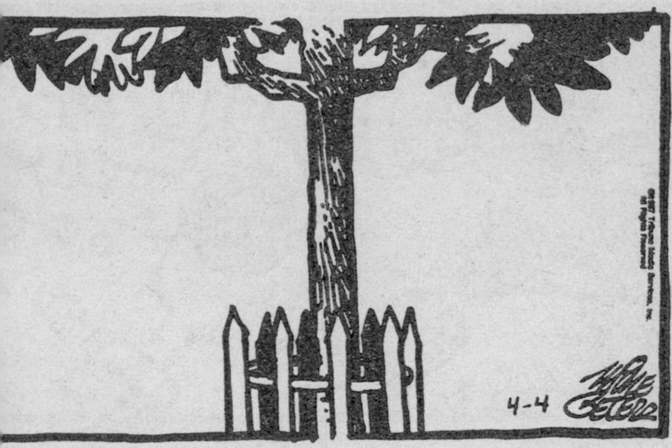
4-4

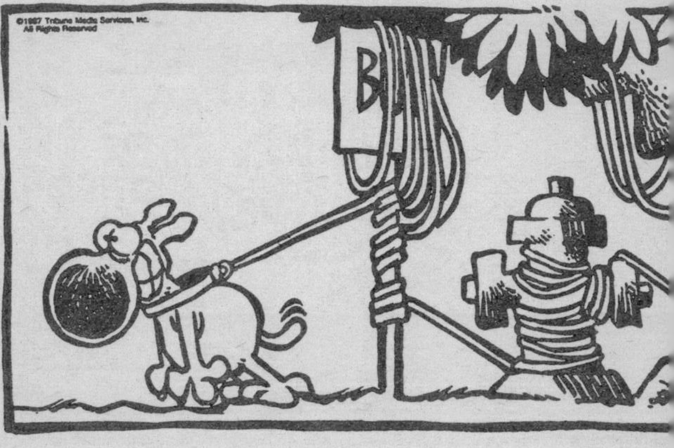
©1987 Tribune Media Services, Inc.
All Rights Reserved

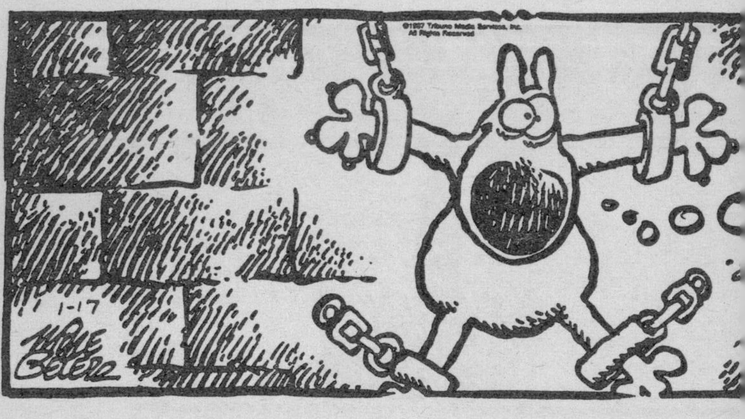
©1987 Tribune Media Services, Inc.
All Rights Reserved
1-17

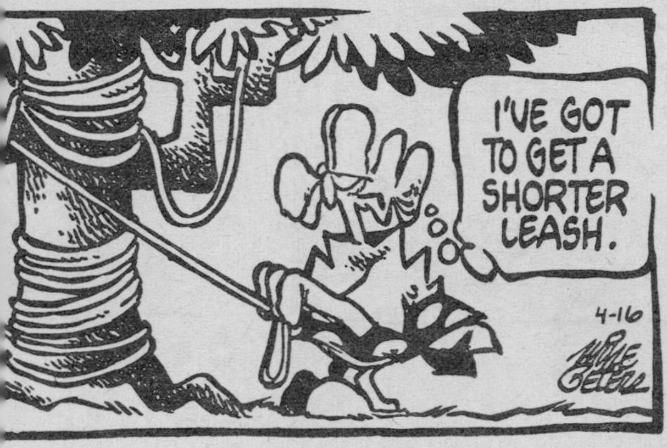
I'VE GOT TO GET A SHORTER LEASH.
4-16
MIKE GELERE

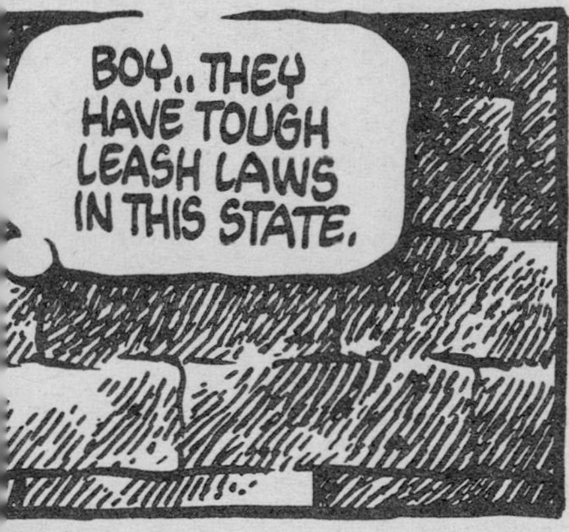
BOY.. THEY HAVE TOUGH LEASH LAWS IN THIS STATE.

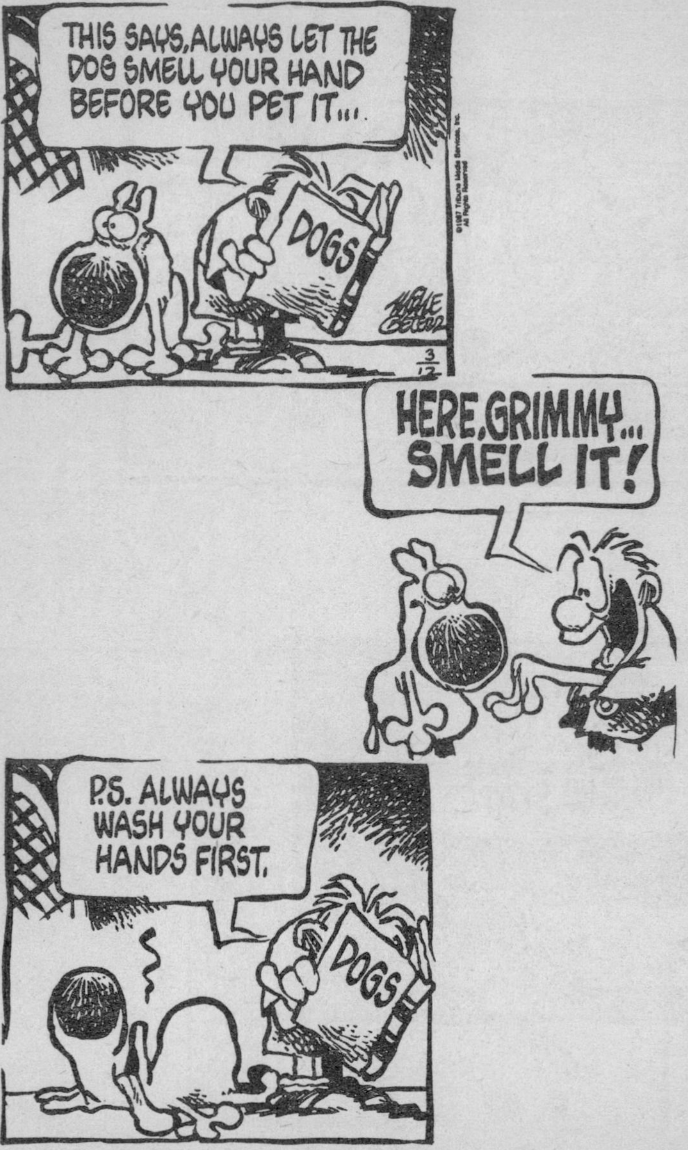
THIS SAYS, ALWAYS LET THE DOG SMELL YOUR HAND BEFORE YOU PET IT...
DOGS
©1987 Tribune Media Services, Inc. All Rights Reserved
3/12
HERE, GRIMMY... SMELL IT!
P.S. ALWAYS WASH YOUR HANDS FIRST.
DOGS

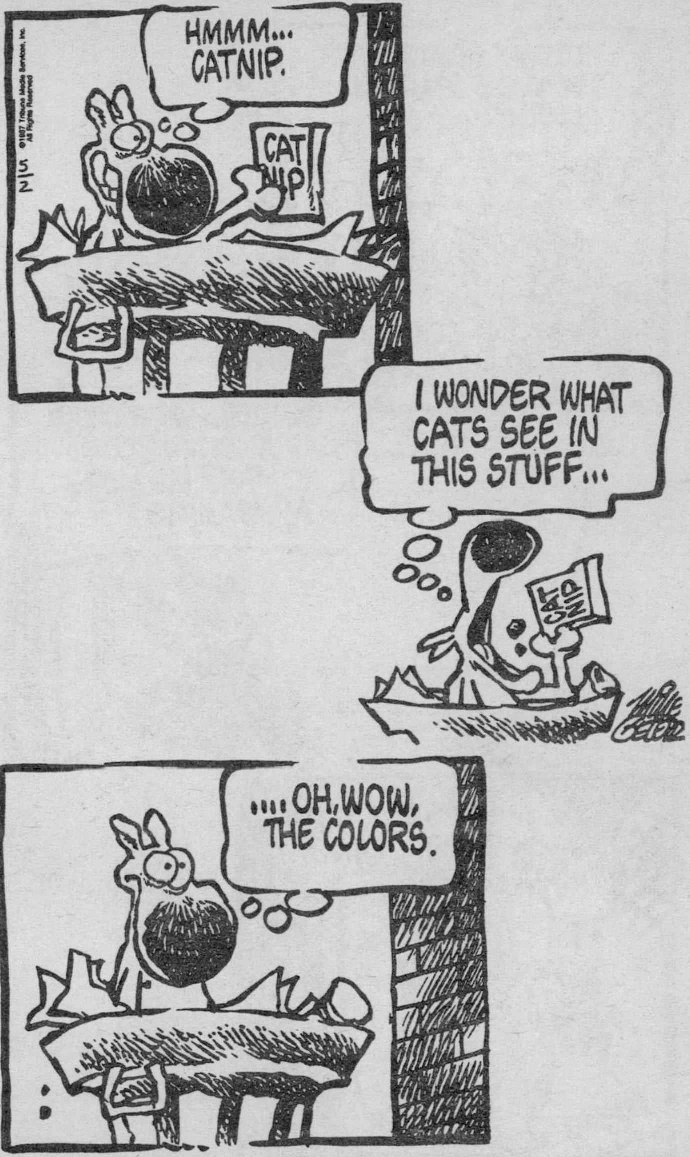
©1997 Tribune Media Services, Inc. All Rights Reserved
HMMM... CATNIP.
CAT NIP
I WONDER WHAT CATS SEE IN THIS STUFF...
CAT NIP
....OH, WOW, THE COLORS.

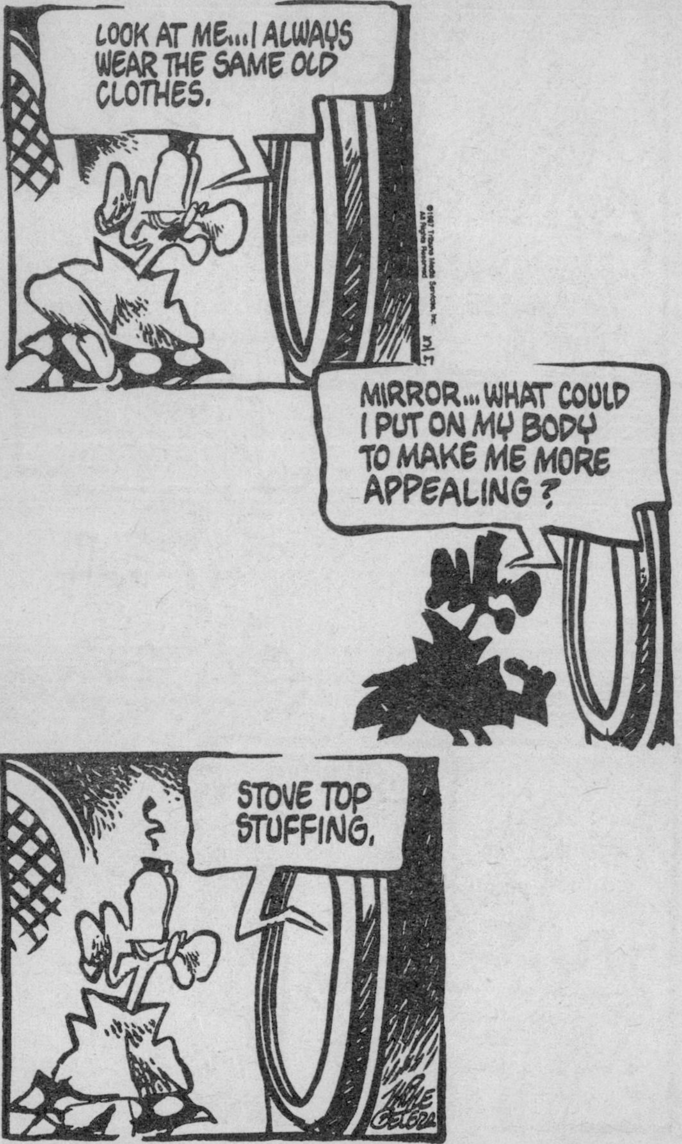
LOOK AT ME...I ALWAYS WEAR THE SAME OLD CLOTHES.
©1987 Tribune Media Services, Inc. All Rights Reserved
MIRROR...WHAT COULD I PUT ON MY BODY TO MAKE ME MORE APPEALING?
STOVE TOP STUFFING.

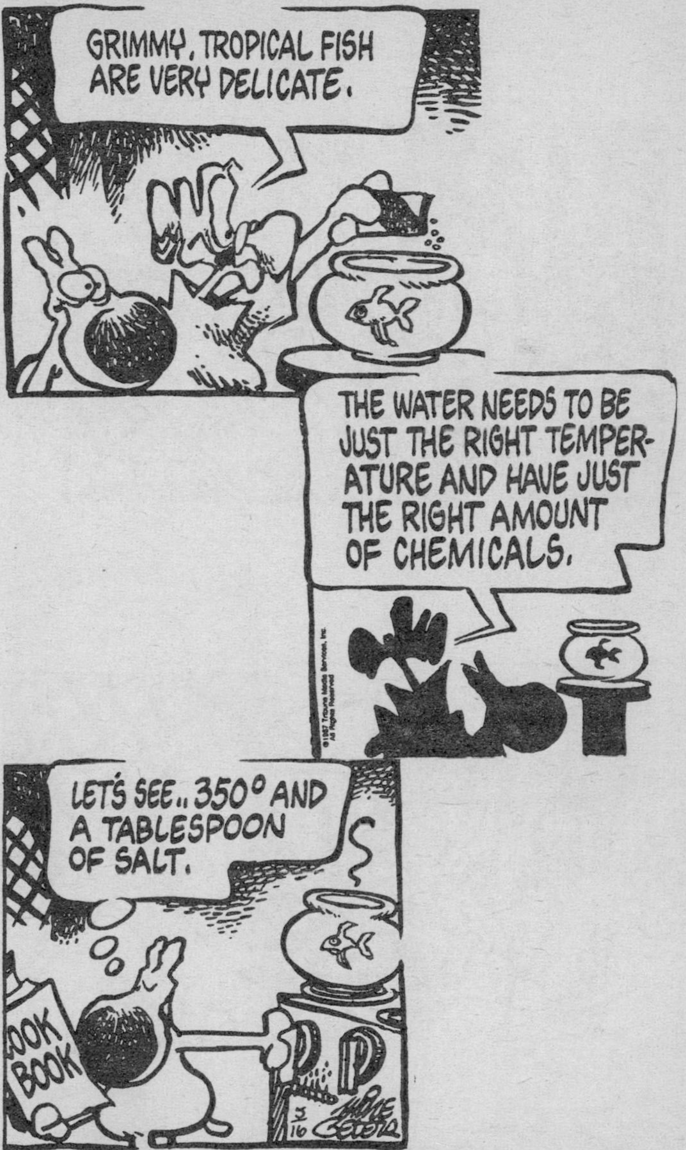

GRIMMY, TROPICAL FISH ARE VERY DELICATE.
THE WATER NEEDS TO BE JUST THE RIGHT TEMPERATURE AND HAVE JUST THE RIGHT AMOUNT OF CHEMICALS.
©1987 Tribune Media Services, Inc. All Rights Reserved
LET'S SEE.. 350° AND A TABLESPOON OF SALT.
OOK BOOK
5/16

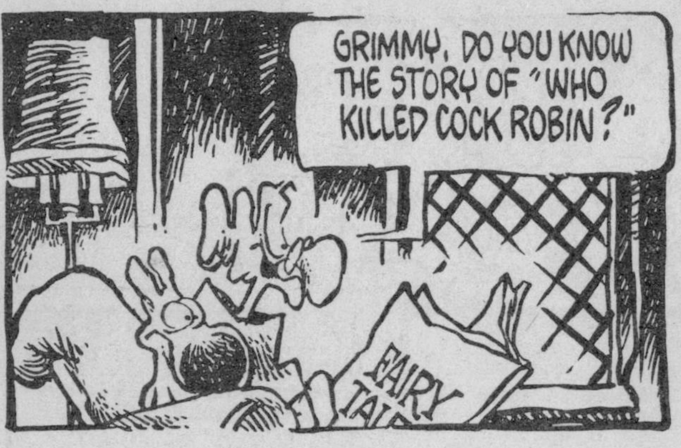
GRIMMY, DO YOU KNOW THE STORY OF "WHO KILLED COCK ROBIN?"
FAIRY TAL

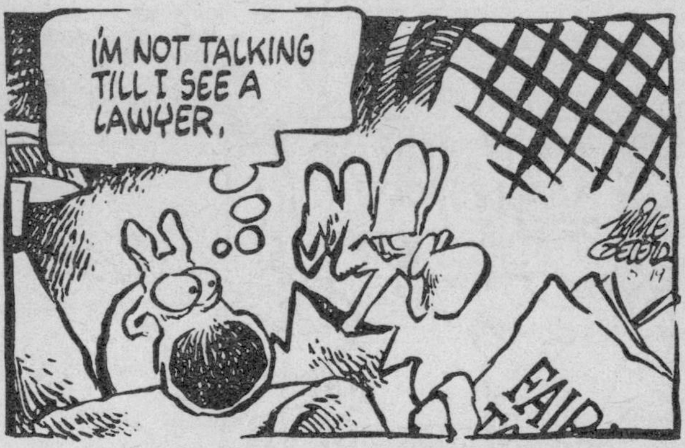
I'M NOT TALKING TILL I SEE A LAWYER.

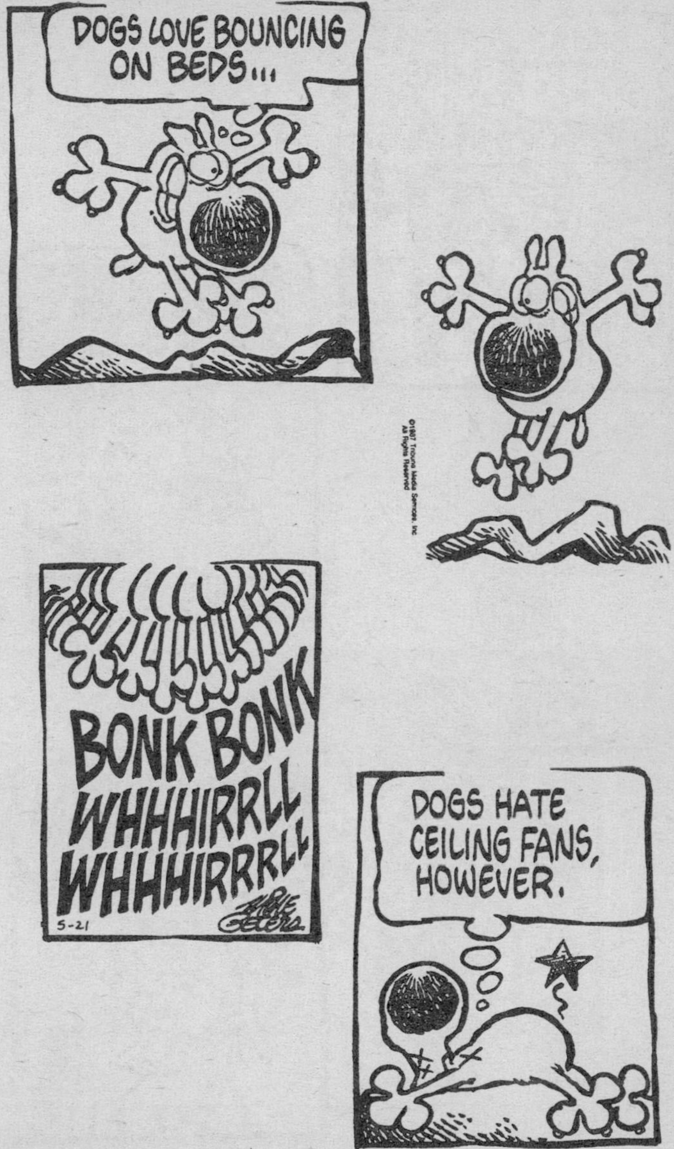
DOGS LOVE BOUNCING ON BEDS...
BONK BONK
WHHHIRRLL
WHHHIRRRLL
5-21
DOGS HATE CEILING FANS, HOWEVER.

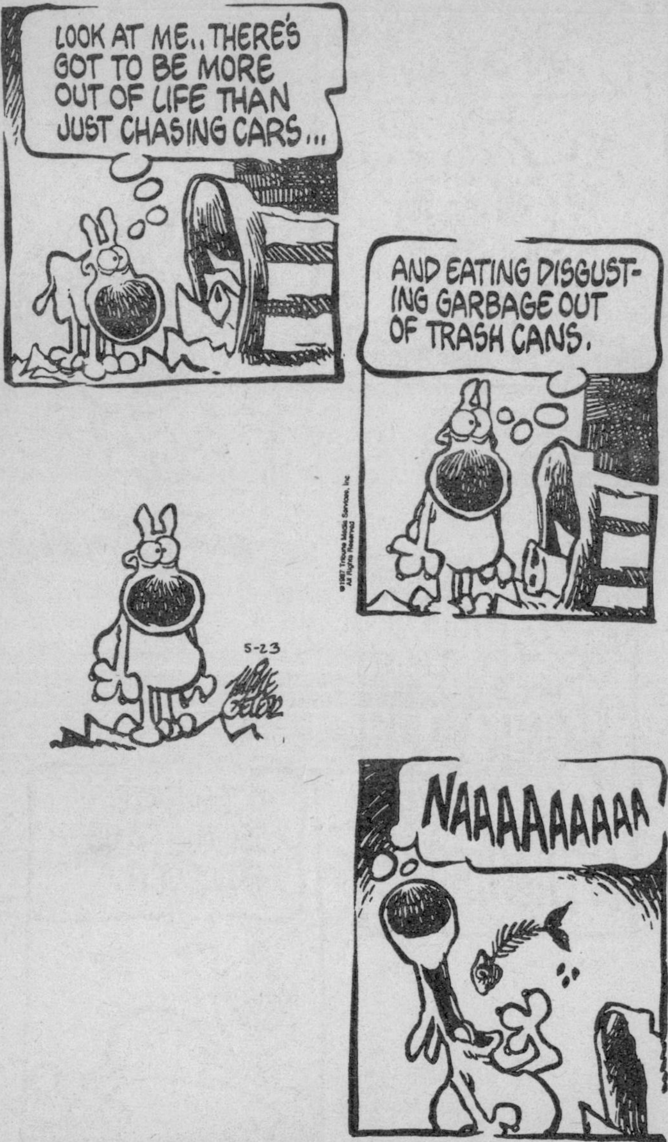
LOOK AT ME.. THERE'S GOT TO BE MORE OUT OF LIFE THAN JUST CHASING CARS...
AND EATING DISGUST-ING GARBAGE OUT OF TRASH CANS.
NAAAAAAAAA
5-23
©1987 Tribune Media Services, Inc
All Rights Reserved

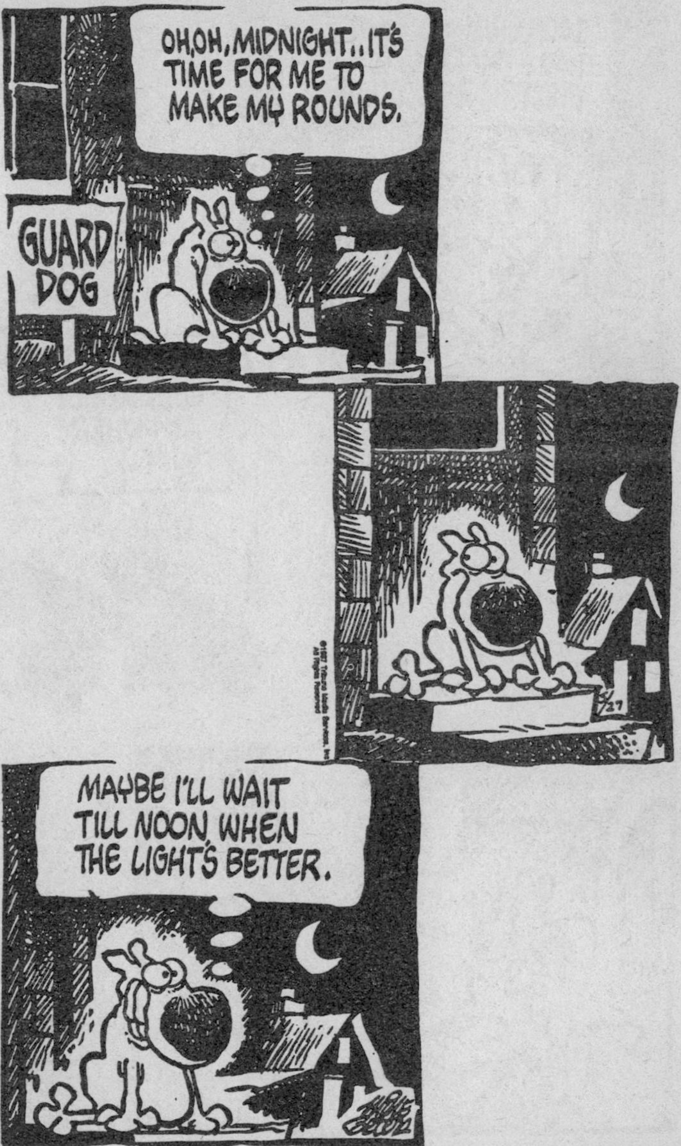
OH,OH, MIDNIGHT...IT'S TIME FOR ME TO MAKE MY ROUNDS.
GUARD DOG
MAYBE I'LL WAIT TILL NOON WHEN THE LIGHT'S BETTER.

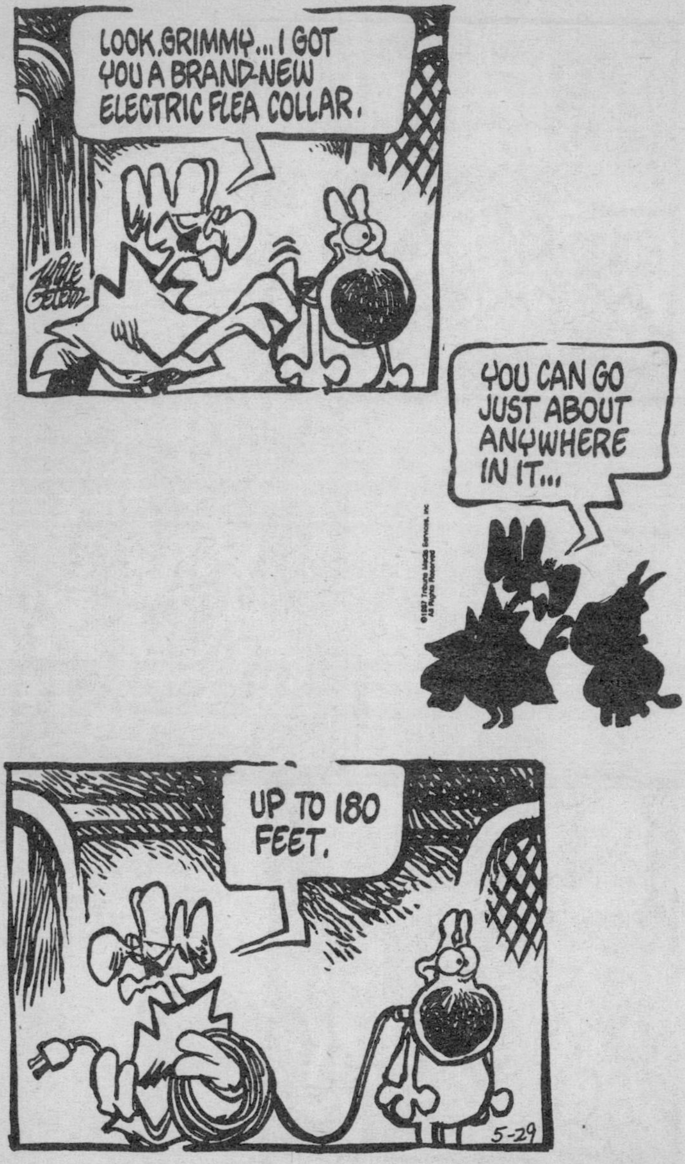
LOOK, GRIMMY... I GOT YOU A BRAND-NEW ELECTRIC FLEA COLLAR.
YOU CAN GO JUST ABOUT ANYWHERE IN IT...
© 1987 Tribune Media Services, Inc All Rights Reserved
UP TO 180 FEET.
5-29

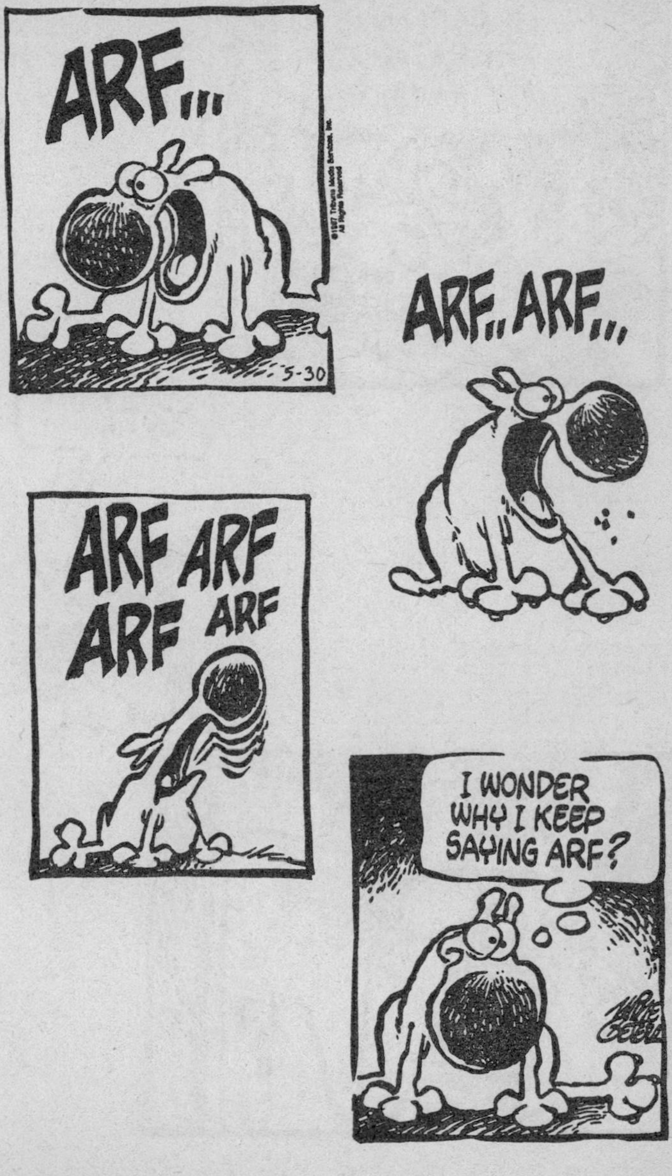

ARF...
©1987 Tribune Media Services, Inc.
All Rights Reserved
5-30
ARF.. ARF...
ARF ARF
ARF ARF
I WONDER WHY I KEEP SAYING ARF?

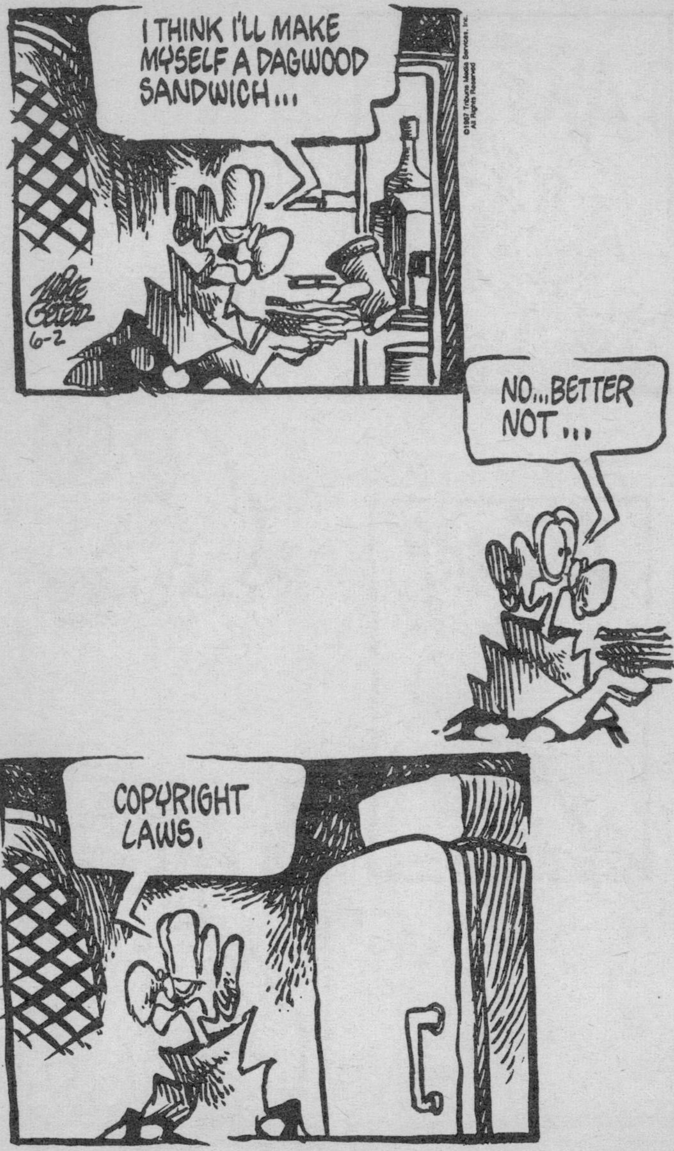
I THINK I'LL MAKE MYSELF A DAGWOOD SANDWICH...
©1987 Tribune Media Services, Inc. All Rights Reserved
6-2
NO...BETTER NOT...
COPYRIGHT LAWS.

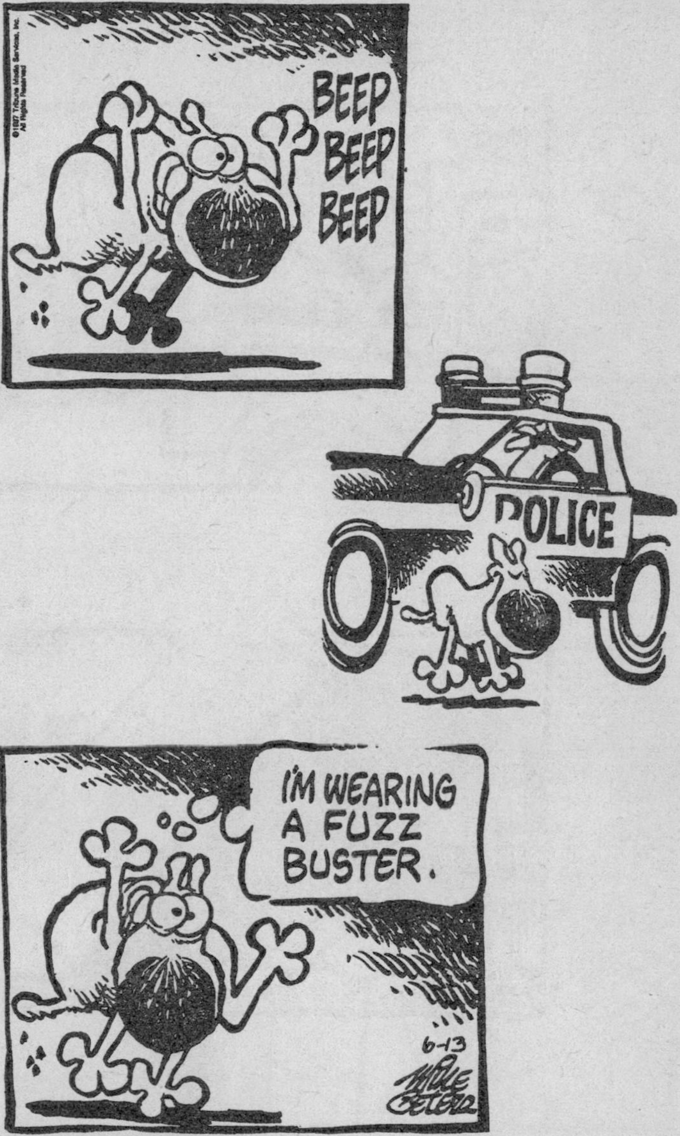
©1987 Tribune Media Services, Inc.
All Rights Reserved
BEEP
BEEP
BEEP
POLICE
I'M WEARING A FUZZ BUSTER.
6-13

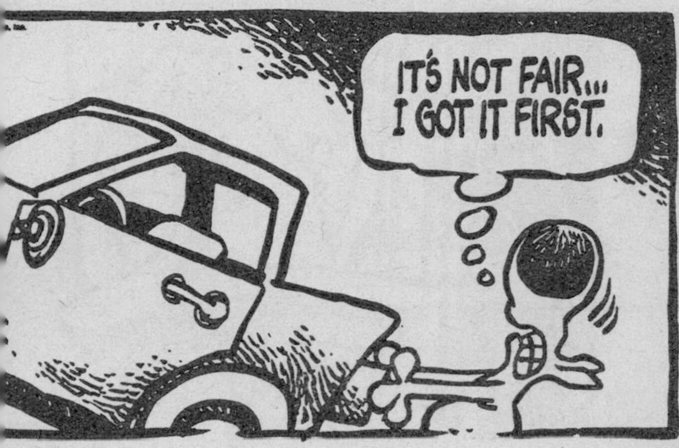
IT'S NOT FAIR...
I GOT IT FIRST.

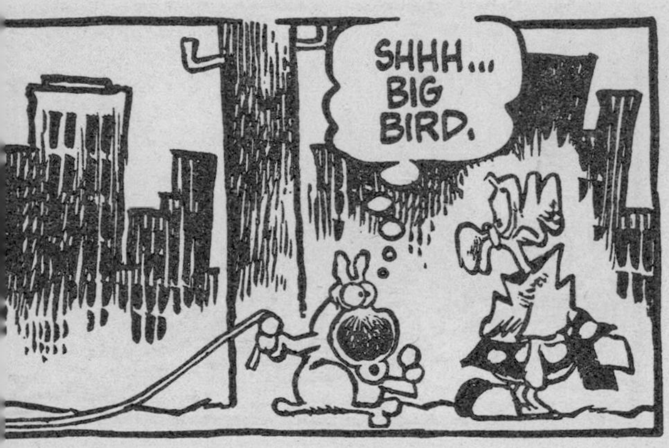
SHHH...
BIG
BIRD.

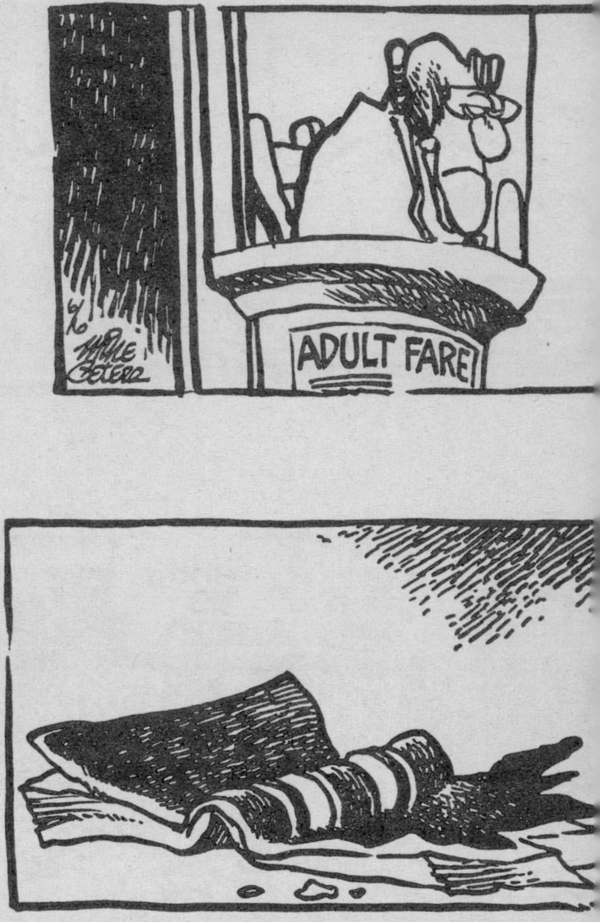
ADULT FARE

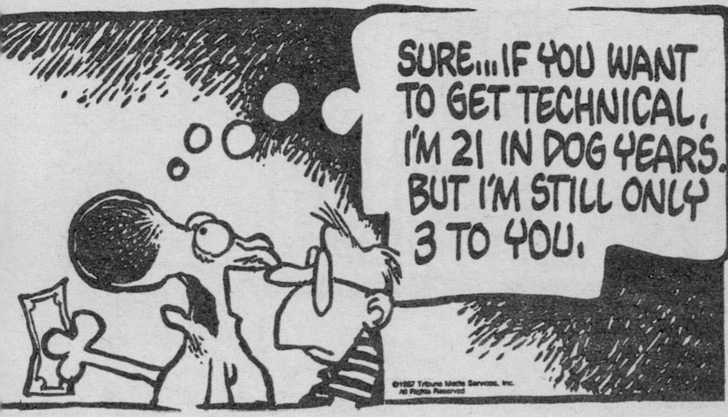
SURE...IF YOU WANT TO GET TECHNICAL, I'M 21 IN DOG YEARS. BUT I'M STILL ONLY 3 TO YOU.
©1997 Tribune Media Services, Inc. All Rights Reserved

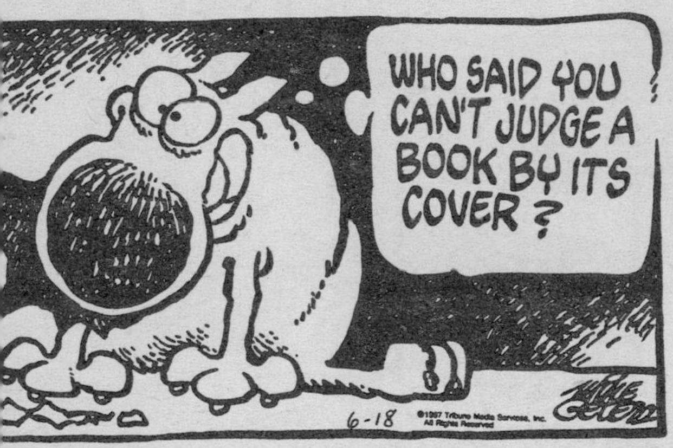
WHO SAID YOU CAN'T JUDGE A BOOK BY ITS COVER?
6-18
©1997 Tribune Media Services, Inc. All Rights Reserved

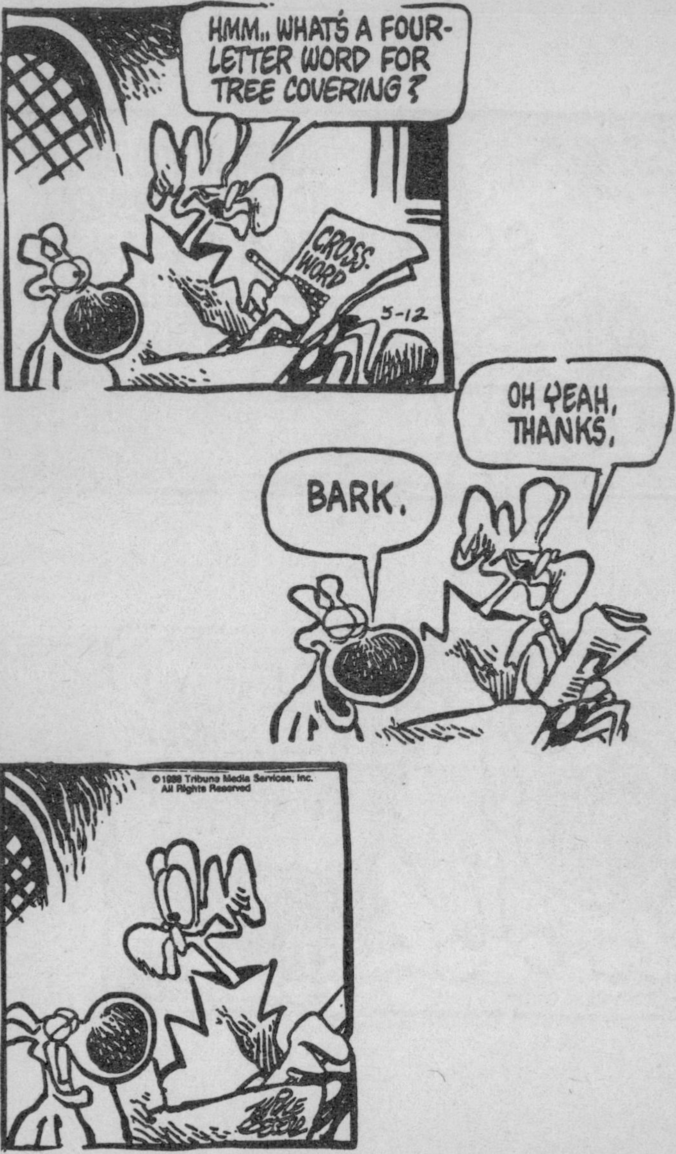
HMM.. WHAT'S A FOUR-LETTER WORD FOR TREE COVERING?
CROSS-WORD
5-12
BARK.
OH YEAH, THANKS.
© 1988 Tribune Media Services, Inc. All Rights Reserved

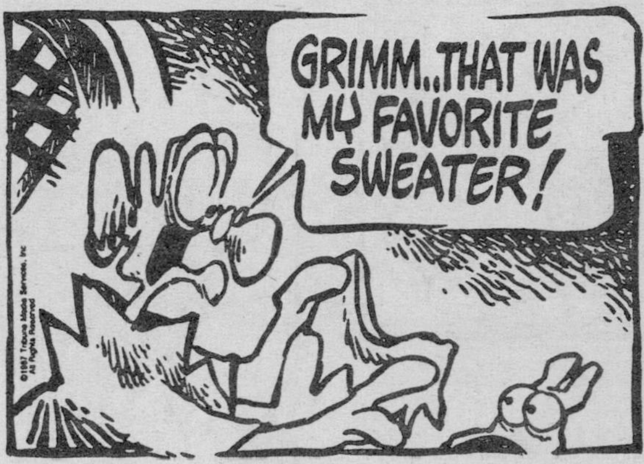
GRIMM..THAT WAS MY FAVORITE SWEATER!
©1987 Tribune Media Services, Inc
All Rights Reserved

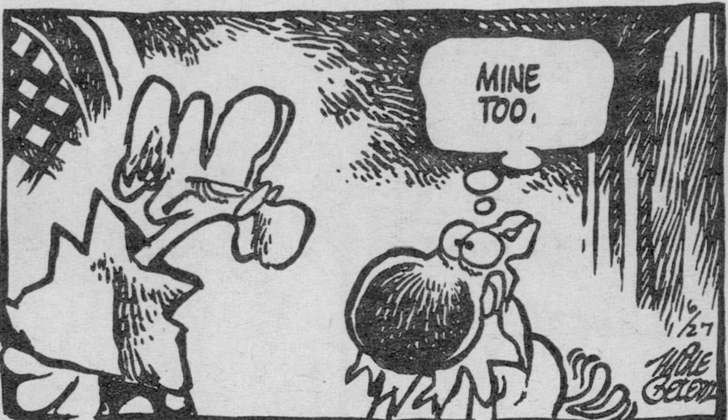
MINE TOO.
6/27

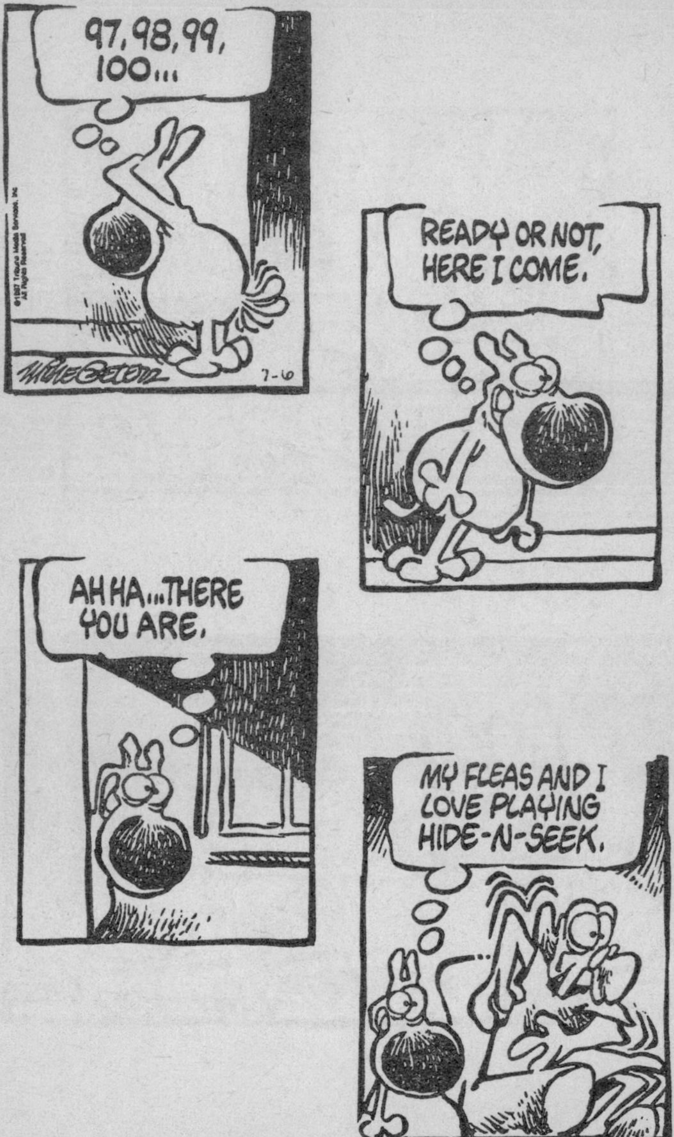

97, 98, 99, 100...
READY OR NOT, HERE I COME.
AH HA...THERE YOU ARE.
MY FLEAS AND I LOVE PLAYING HIDE-N-SEEK.

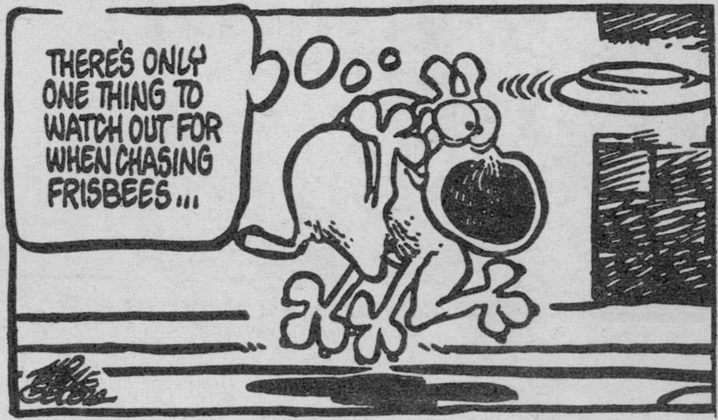
THERE'S ONLY ONE THING TO WATCH OUT FOR WHEN CHASING FRISBEES...

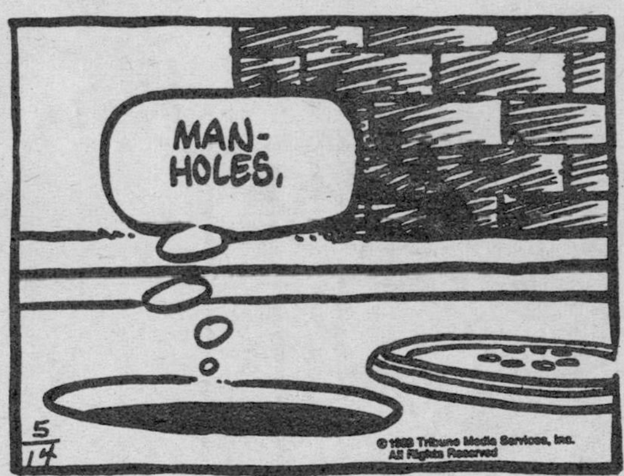
MAN-HOLES.
5/14
Tribune Media Services, Inc.
All Rights Reserved

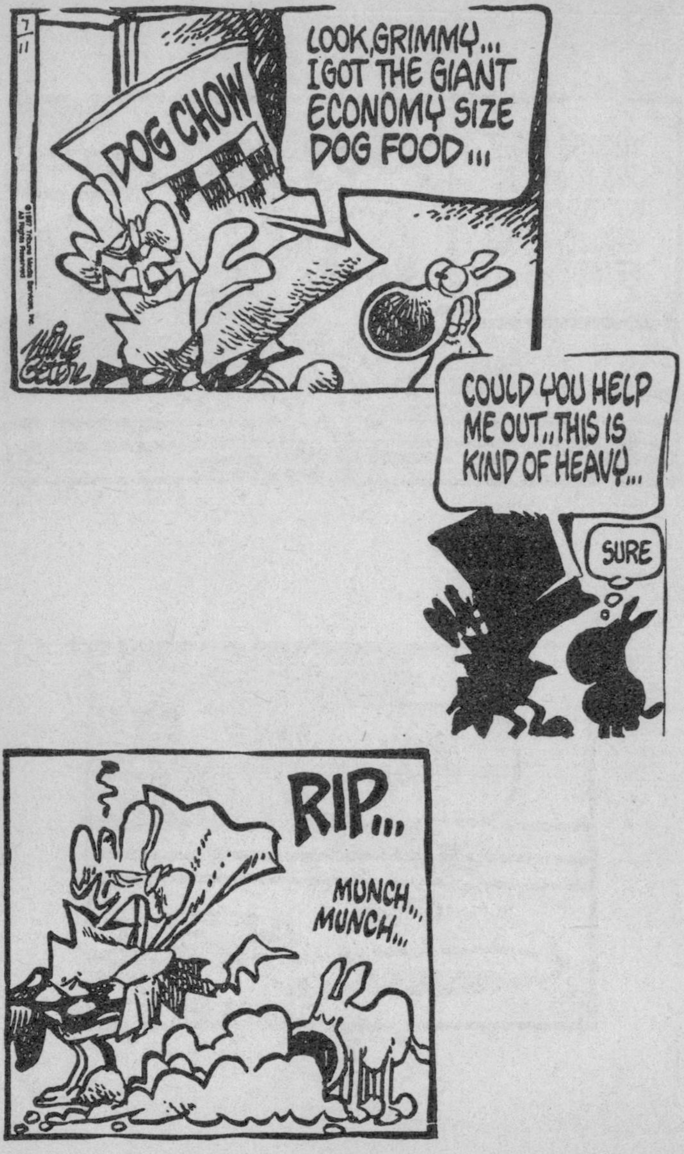
7/11
LOOK, GRIMMY... I GOT THE GIANT ECONOMY SIZE DOG FOOD...
DOG CHOW
COULD YOU HELP ME OUT,,THIS IS KIND OF HEAVY...
SURE
RIP...
MUNCH,,, MUNCH,,,

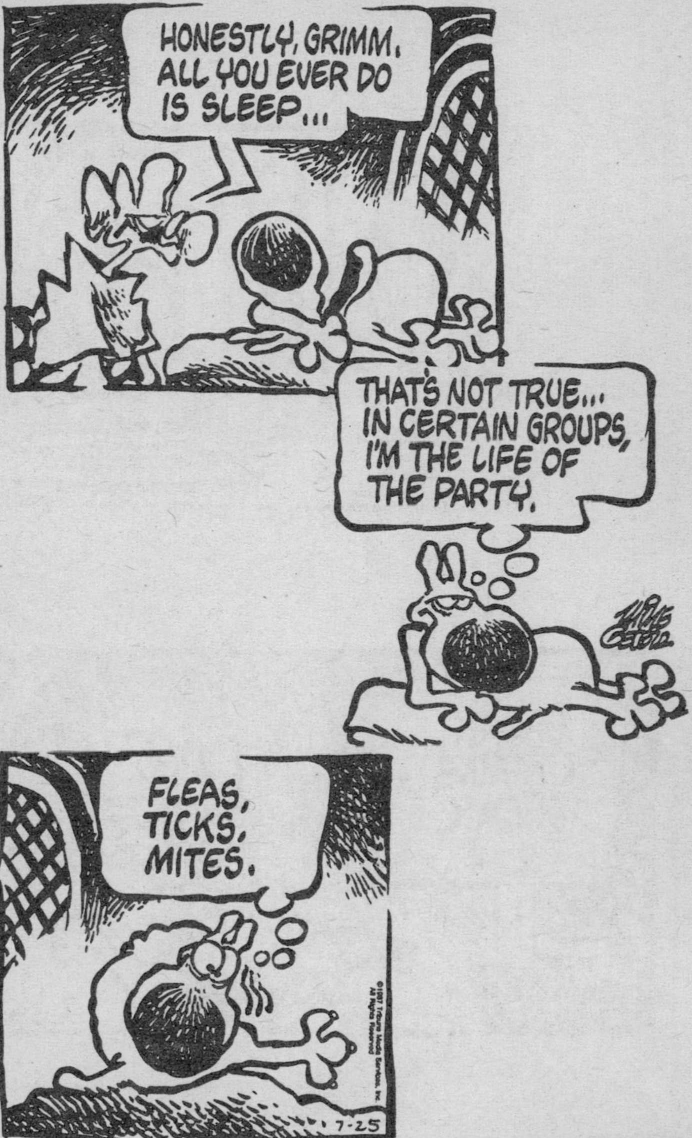
HONESTLY, GRIMM. ALL YOU EVER DO IS SLEEP...
THAT'S NOT TRUE... IN CERTAIN GROUPS, I'M THE LIFE OF THE PARTY.
FLEAS, TICKS, MITES.
©1987 Tribune Media Services, Inc. All Rights Reserved
7-25

SPEAK, GRIMMY, SPEAK,

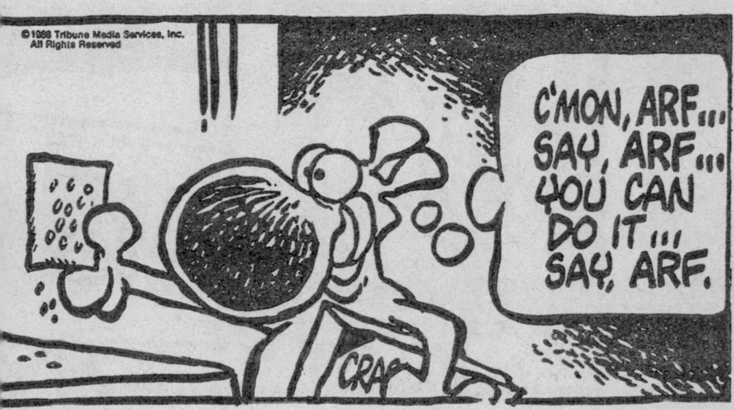
©1988 Tribune Media Services, Inc.
All Rights Reserved
C'MON, ARF... SAY, ARF... YOU CAN DO IT... SAY, ARF.
CRAP

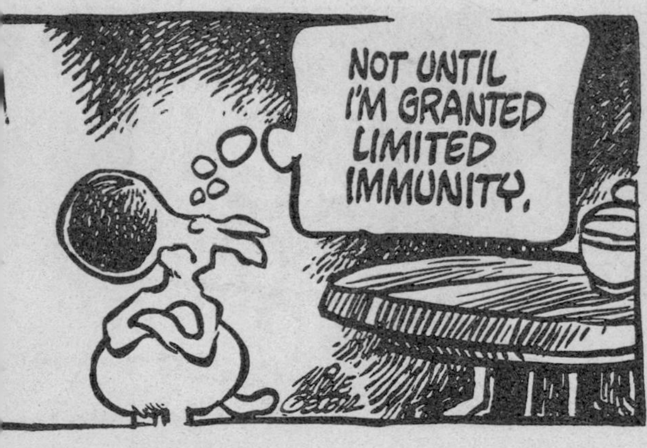
NOT UNTIL I'M GRANTED LIMITED IMMUNITY.

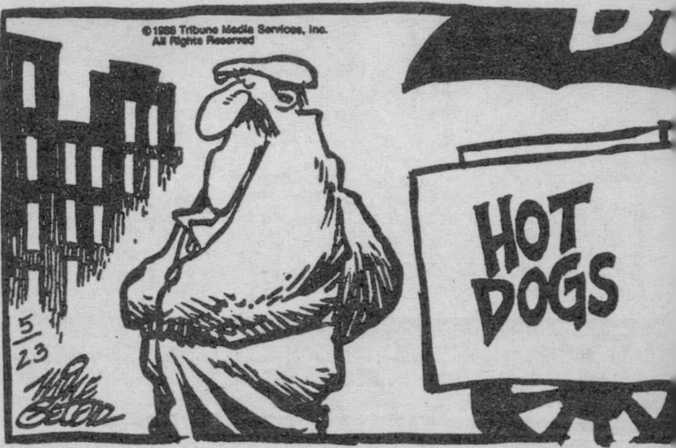
©1988 Tribune Media Services, Inc.
All Rights Reserved
HOT
DOGS
5/23

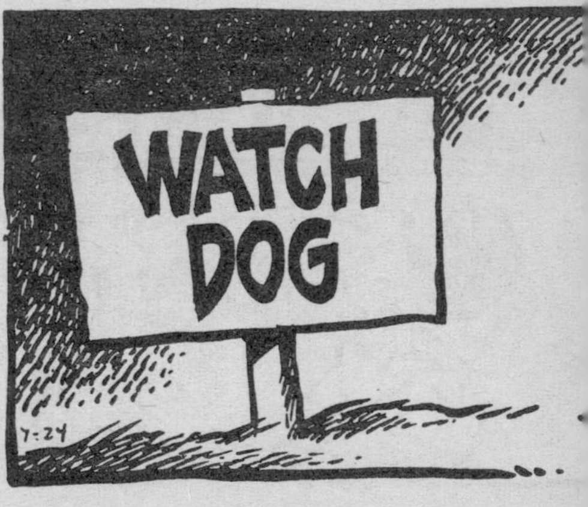
WATCH
DOG
7-24

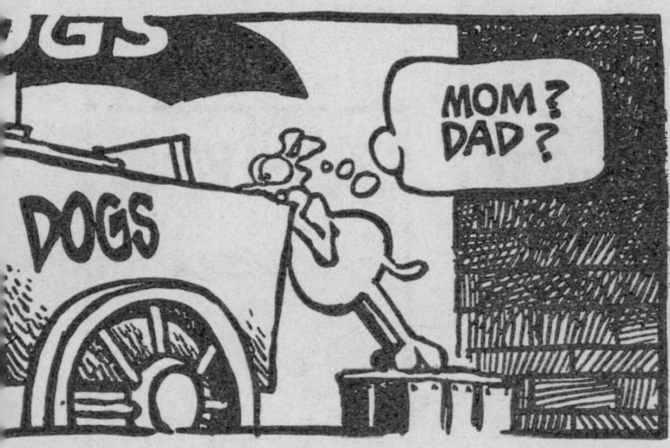
MOM?
DAD?

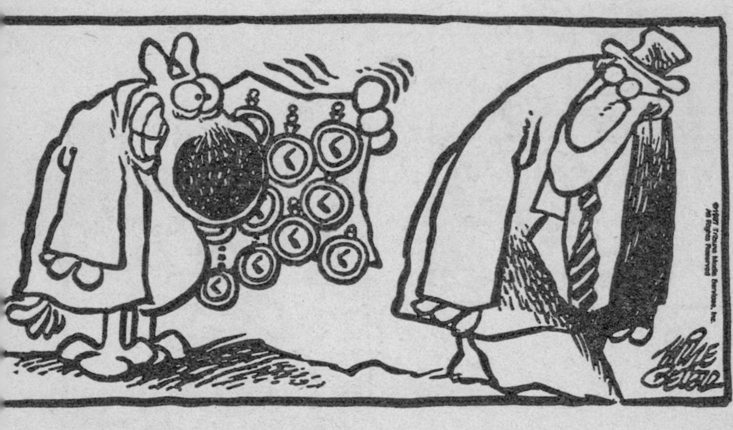
Tribune Media Services, Inc.
All Rights Reserved

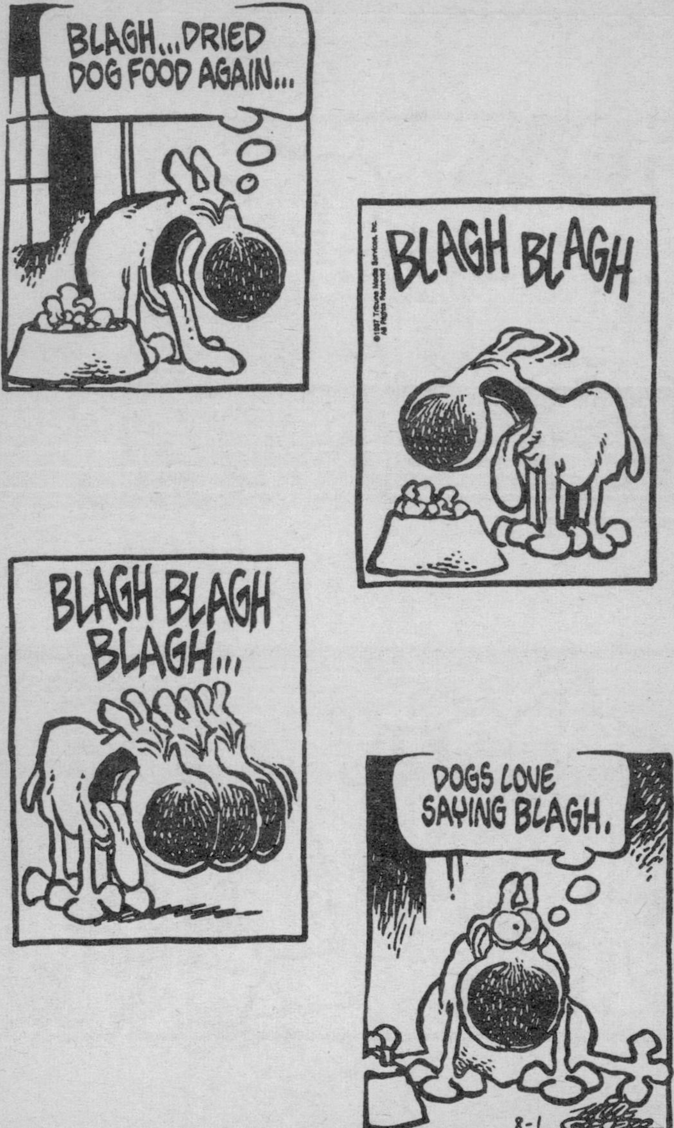
BLAGH...DRIED DOG FOOD AGAIN...
BLAGH BLAGH
©1997 Tribune Media Services, Inc.
All Rights Reserved
BLAGH BLAGH BLAGH...
DOGS LOVE SAYING BLAGH.
8-1

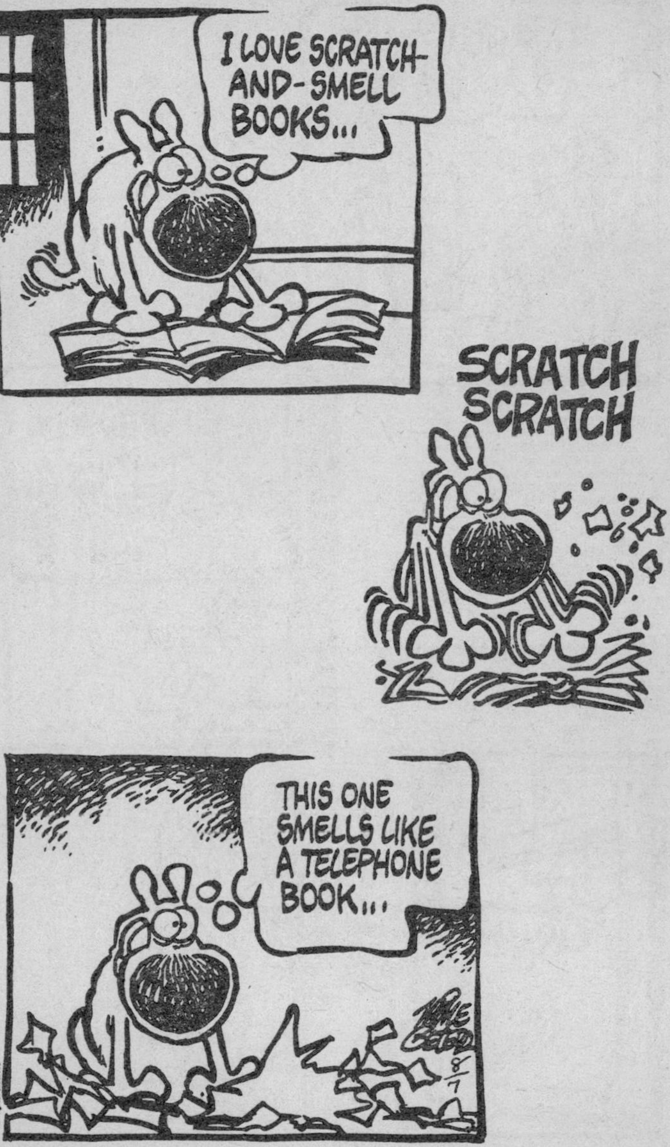
I LOVE SCRATCH-AND-SMELL BOOKS...
SCRATCH SCRATCH
THIS ONE SMELLS LIKE A TELEPHONE BOOK...

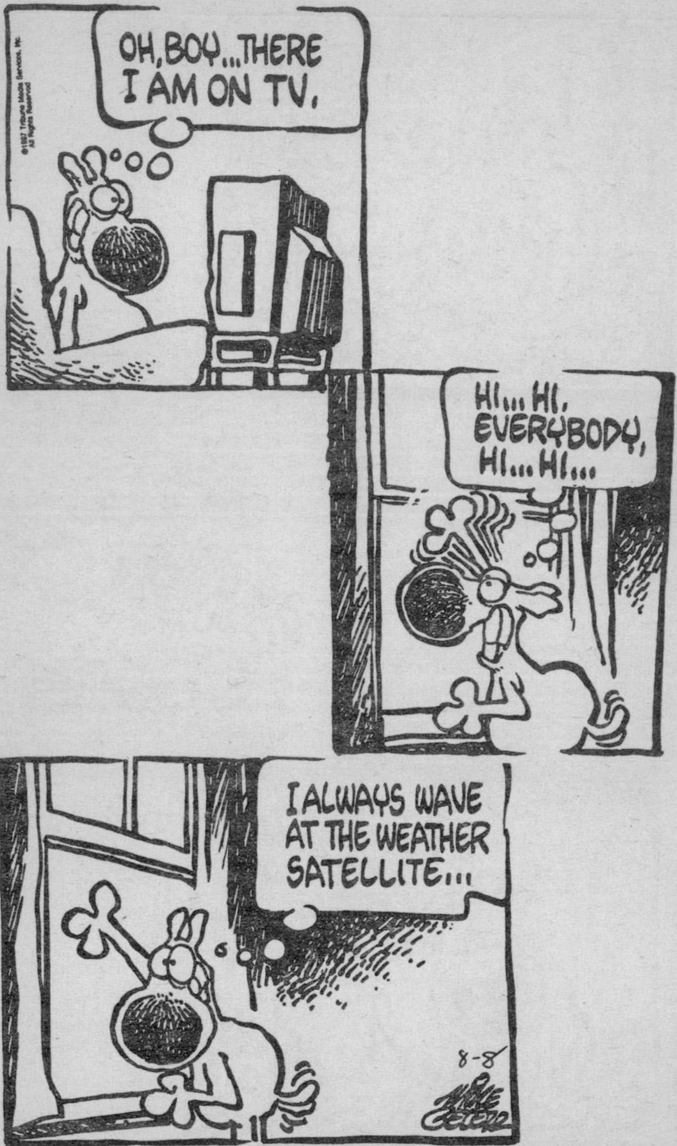
©1987 Tribune Media Services, Inc.
All Rights Reserved
OH, BOY... THERE I AM ON TV.
HI... HI, EVERYBODY, HI... HI...
I ALWAYS WAVE AT THE WEATHER SATELLITE...
8-8

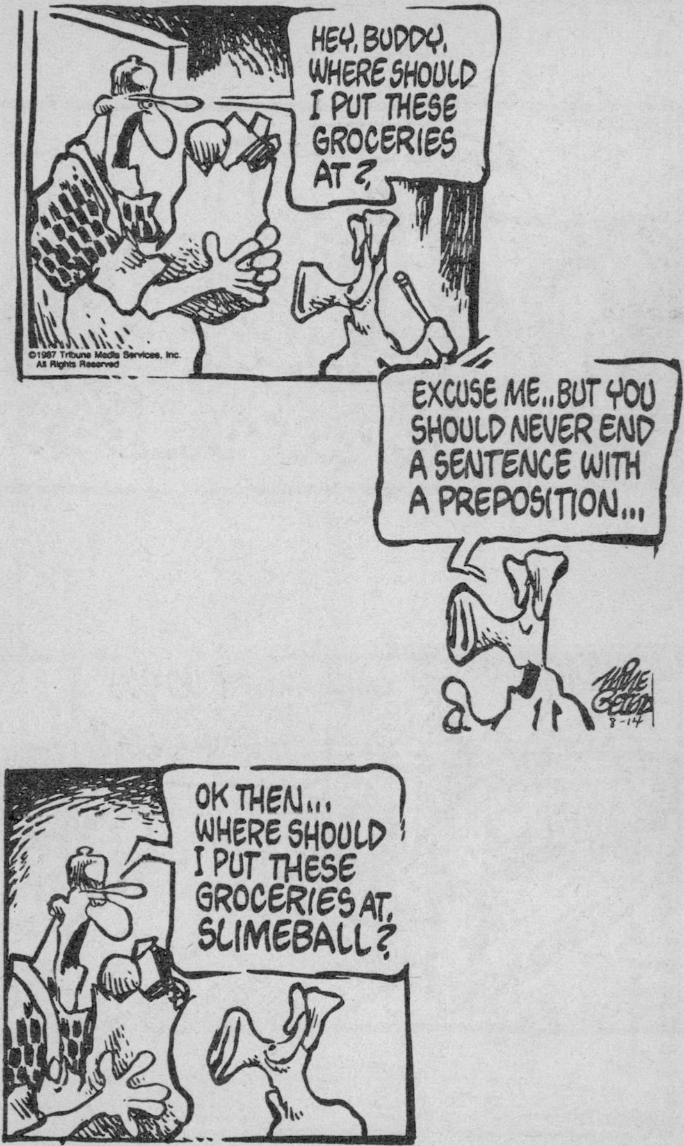

HEY, BUDDY. WHERE SHOULD I PUT THESE GROCERIES AT?
©1987 Tribune Media Services, Inc. All Rights Reserved
EXCUSE ME.. BUT YOU SHOULD NEVER END A SENTENCE WITH A PREPOSITION...
OK THEN... WHERE SHOULD I PUT THESE GROCERIES AT, SLIMEBALL?

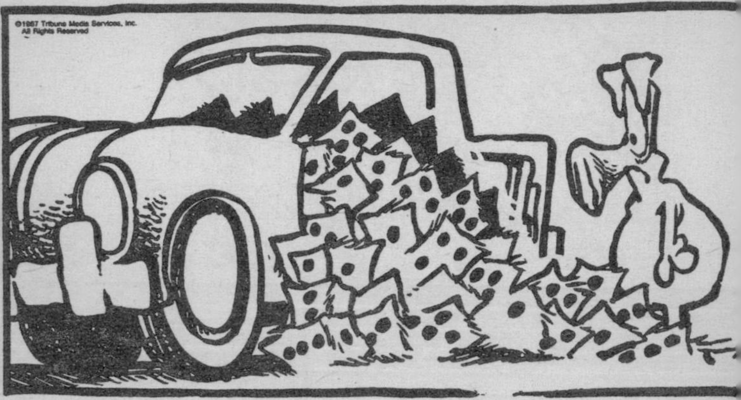
©1987 Tribune Media Services, Inc.
All Rights Reserved

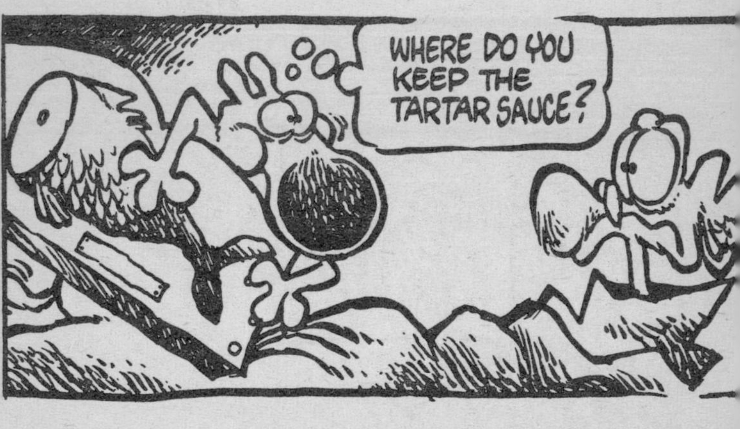
WHERE DO YOU KEEP THE TARTAR SAUCE?

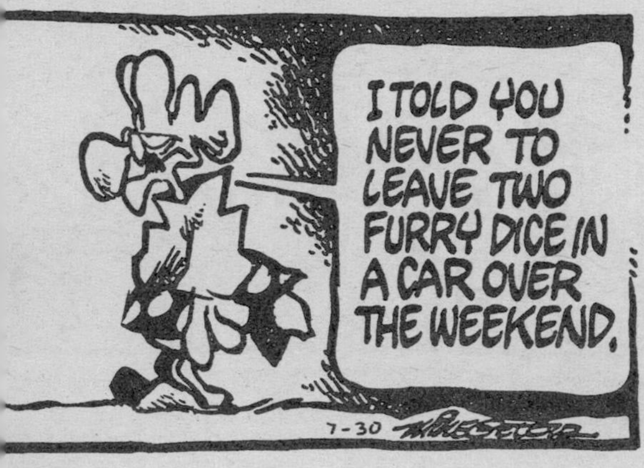
I TOLD YOU NEVER TO LEAVE TWO FURRY DICE IN A CAR OVER THE WEEKEND.
7-30

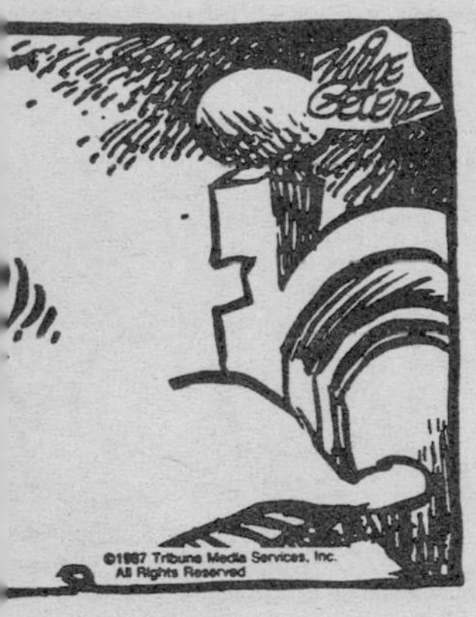
©1987 Tribune Media Services, Inc.
All Rights Reserved

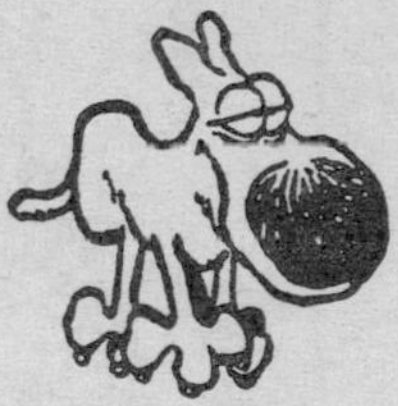

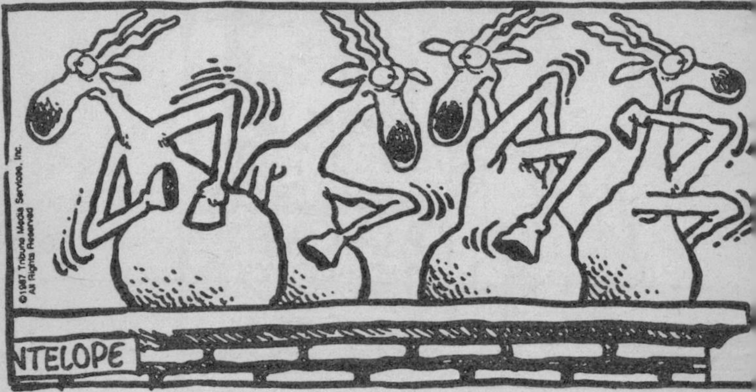
NTELOPE
©1987 Tribune Media Services, Inc.
All Rights Reserved

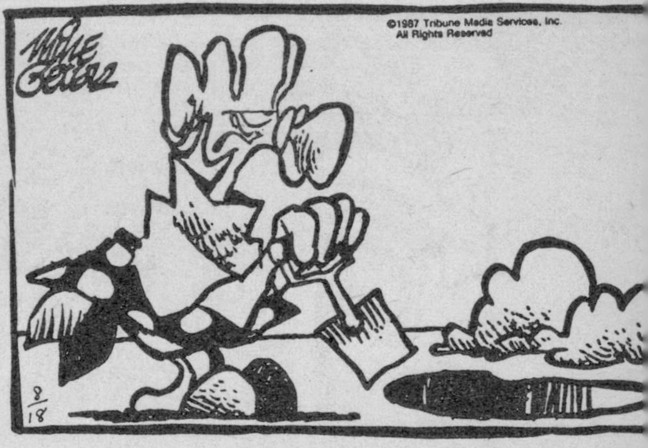
©1987 Tribune Media Services, Inc.
All Rights Reserved
8/18

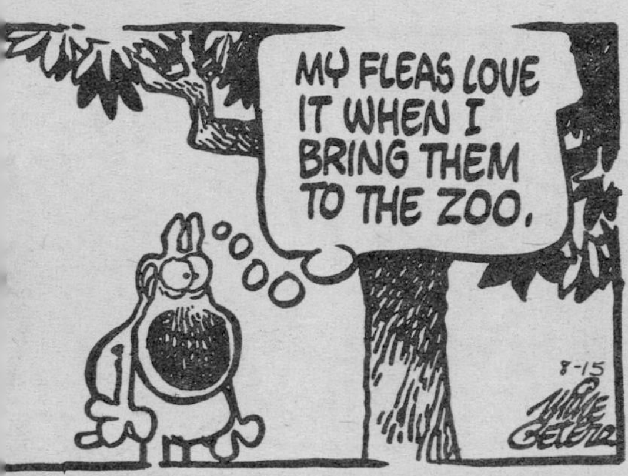
MY FLEAS LOVE IT WHEN I BRING THEM TO THE ZOO.
8-15
Mike Peters
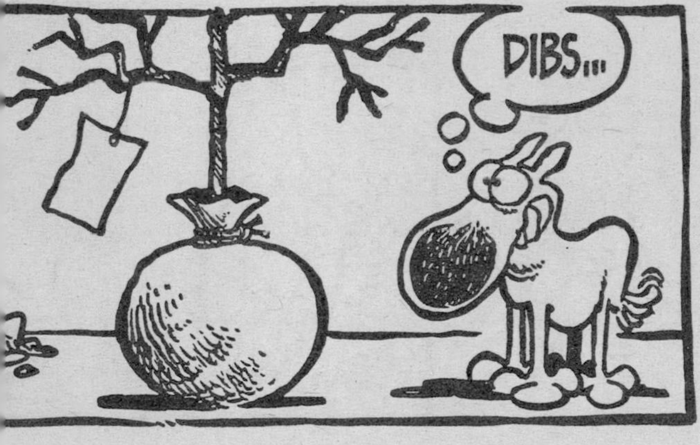
DIBS...

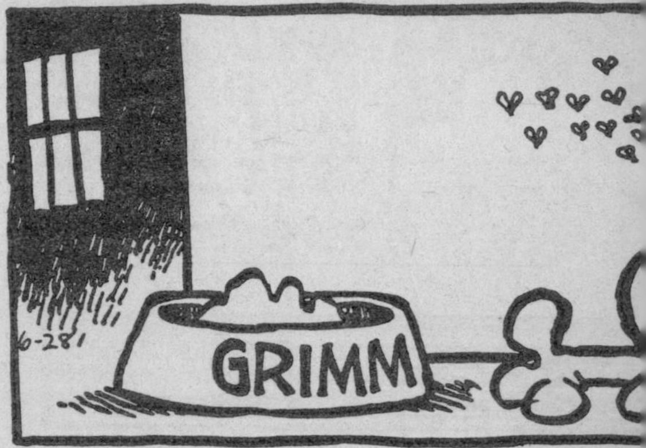
6-28
GRIMM

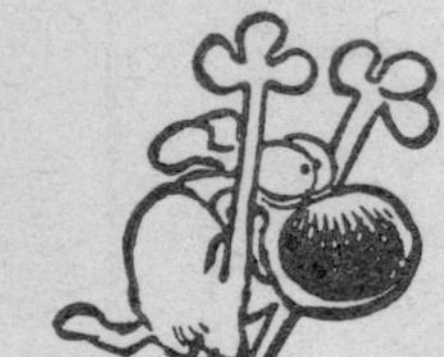

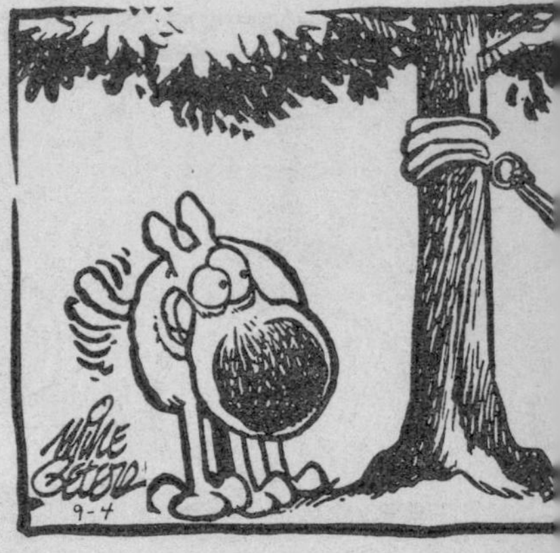
MIKE PETERS
9-4

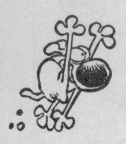

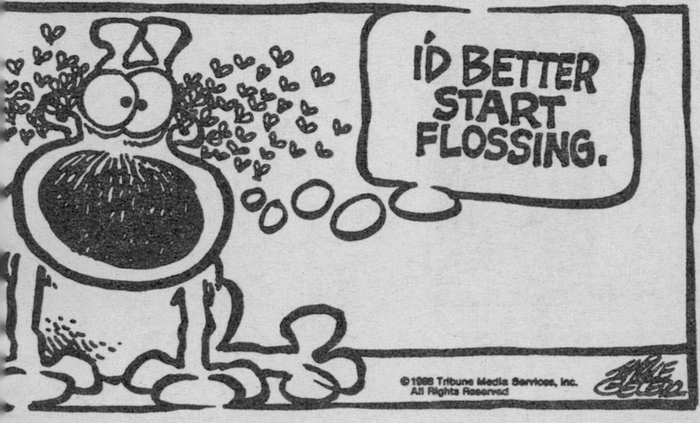

I'D BETTER START FLOSSING.
©1988 Tribune Media Services, Inc.
All Rights Reserved

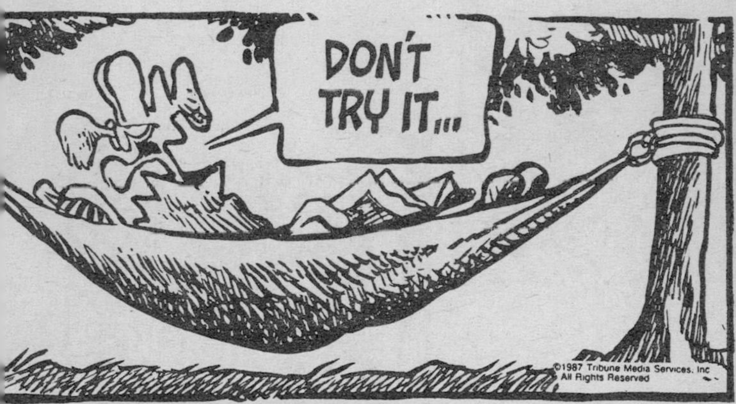

DON'T TRY IT...
©1987 Tribune Media Services, Inc
All Rights Reserved

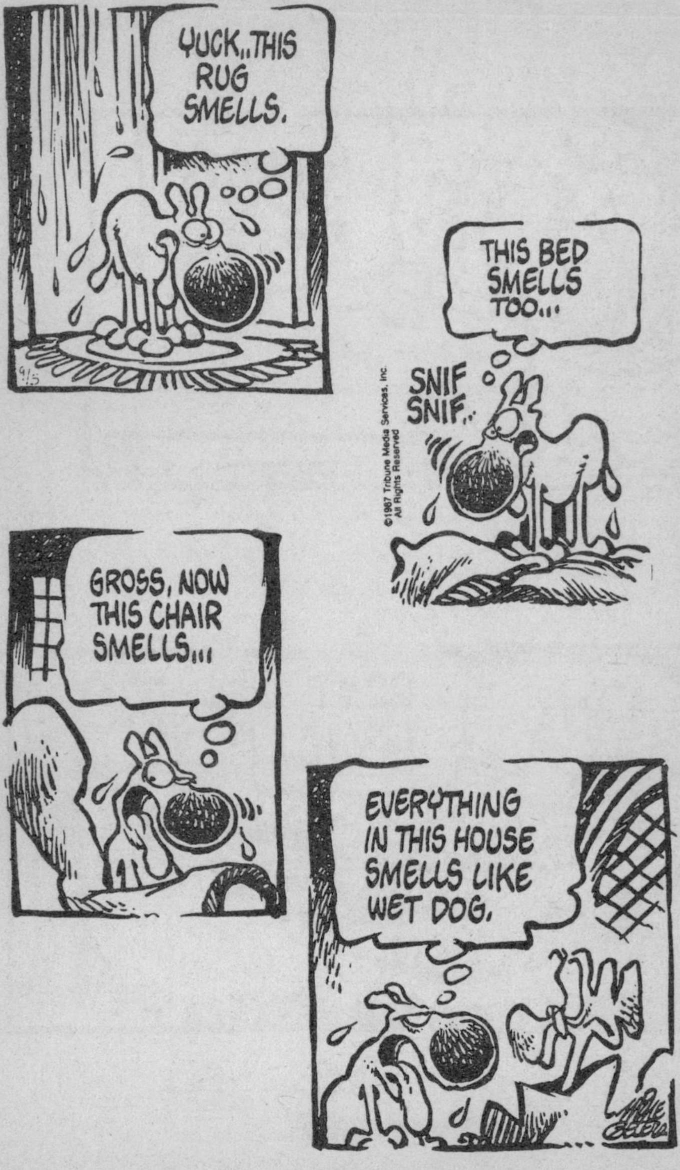
YUCK,,THIS RUG SMELLS.
9/5
THIS BED SMELLS TOO...
SNIF SNIF..
GROSS, NOW THIS CHAIR SMELLS...
EVERYTHING IN THIS HOUSE SMELLS LIKE WET DOG.
MIKE PETERS

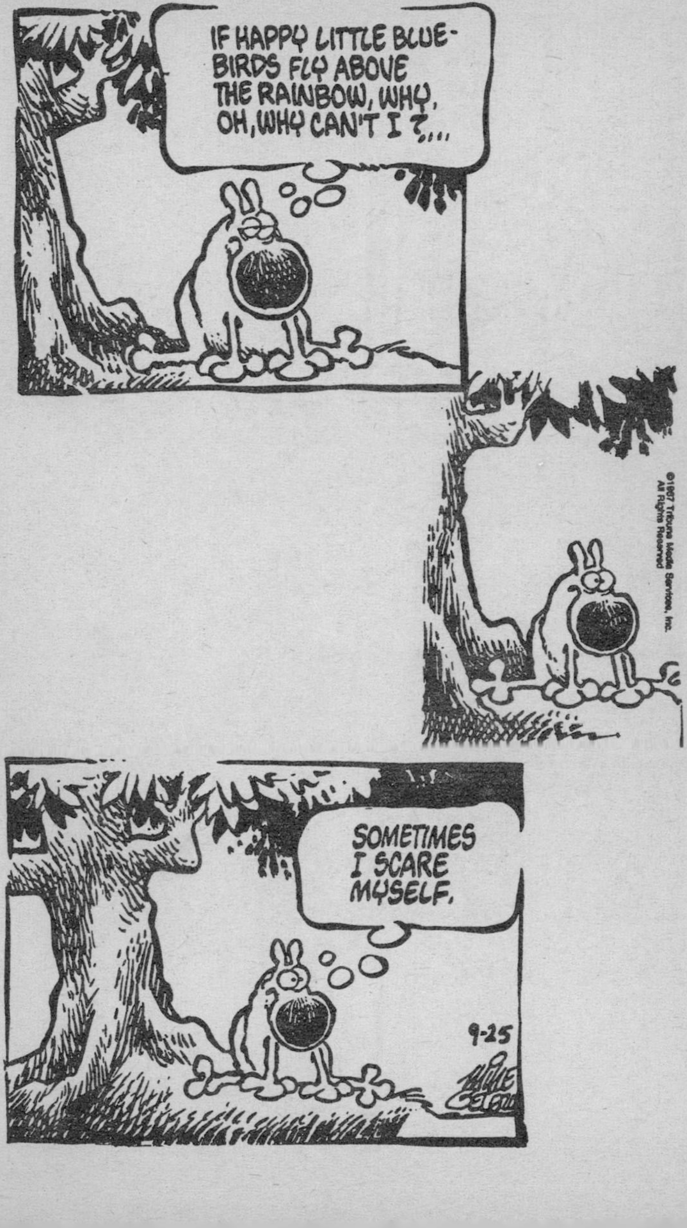
IF HAPPY LITTLE BLUE-BIRDS FLY ABOVE THE RAINBOW, WHY, OH, WHY CAN'T I ?...
©1987 Tribune Media Services, Inc. All Rights Reserved
SOMETIMES I SCARE MYSELF.
9-25